THE PRIZE STORIES

OTHER INDIAN EXPRESS TITLES:

Indian Express	*The Prize Stories: Best in the Indian News Business 2005-2006*
Indian Express	*The Prize Stories: Best in the Indian News Business 2006-2007*

OTHER LOTUS TITLES

Ajit Bhattacharjea	*Sheikh Mohammad Abdullah: Tragic Hero of Kashmir*
Anil Dharker	*Icons: Men & Women Who Shaped Today's India*
Aitzaz Ahsan	*The Indus Saga: The Making of Pakistan*
Alam Srinivas & TR Vivek	*IPL: The Inside Story*
Amarinder Singh	*The Last Sunset: The Rise & Fall of the Lahore Durbar*
Amir Mir	*The True Face of Jehadis: Inside Pakistan's Terror Networks*
Ashok Mitra	*The Starkness of It*
H.L.O. Garrett	*The Trial of Bahadur Shah Zafar*
L.S. Rathore	*The Regal Patriot: The Maharaja Ganga Singh of Bikaner*
M.B. Naqvi	*Pakistan at Knife's Edge*
M.J. Akbar	*Byline*
M.J. Akbar	*Blood Brothers: A Family Saga*
Maj. Gen. Ian Cardozo	*Param Vir: Our Heroes in Battle*
Maj. Gen. Ian Cardozo	*The Sinking of INS Khukri: What Happened in 1971*
Madhu Trehan	*Tehelka as Metaphor*
Nayantara Sahgal (ed.)	*Before Freedom: Nehru's Letters to His Sister*
Nilima Lambah	*A Life Across Three Continents*
Peter Church	*Added Value: The Life Stories of Indian Business Leaders*
Sharmishta Gooptu and Boria Majumdar (eds)	*Revisiting 1857: Myth, Memory, History*
Shashi Joshi	*The Last Durbar*
Shashi Tharoor & Shaharyar M. Khan	*Shadows Across the Playing Field*
Shrabani Basu	*Spy Princess: The Life of Noor Inayat Khan*
Shyam Bhatia	*Goodbye Shahzadi: A Political Biography*
Vir Sanghvi	*Men of Steel: Indian Business Leaders in Candid Conversations*

FORTHCOMING TITLES

M.J. Akbar	*Have Pen, Will Travel*
Michel De Grece	*The Bourbon Rajah*

THE PRIZE STORIES

BEST IN THE INDIAN NEWS BUSINESS

2007-2008

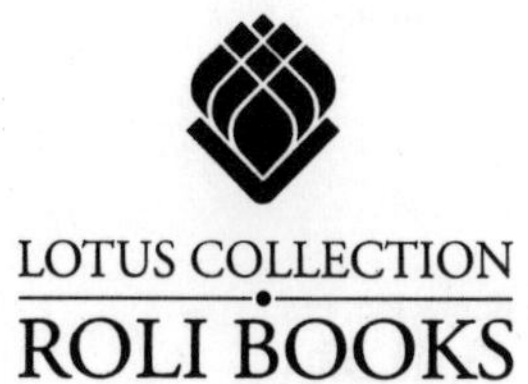

Lotus Collection

Courtesy: *Business World, Financial Times, Lokmat, Madhyamam Daily, Pratham Pravakta, Tehelka, The Hindu, The Hindustan Times*, and *The Week*.

We thank Shailaja Bajpai, Consulting Editor, The Indian Express *for editorial assistance. Also our thanks to Ambreen Khan, Pankaj Bhutani & Neeraj Priyadarshi of* The Indian Express *for their assistance.*

First published in 2010
The Lotus Collection
An imprint of
Roli Books Pvt. Ltd
M-75, Greater Kailash II Market, New Delhi 110 048
Phone: ++91 (011) 4068 2000
Fax: ++91 (011) 2921 7185
E-mail: info@rolibooks.com; Website: www.rolibooks.com
Also at
Bangalore, Chennai, Jaipur, Mumbai & Varanasi

Photograph courtesy: The Express Group

ISBN: 978-81-7436-808-9

Typeset in MinionPro by Roli Books Pvt. Ltd
Printed at Ana Print O Grafix Pvt. Ltd, Delhi

CONTENTS

Foreword – Viveck Goenka 7

Introduction – KG Balakrishnan 9

Is the Line Blurring Between Journalism and Politics – A Panel Discussion 12

DABBA TRADING – Abhishek Upadhyay 21

AIDS ORPHANS' STORY – Dnyanesh V Jathar 25

RADICAL THINKING – Joseph Johnson 39

A CRITIQUE OF TELEVISION NEWS – Karan Thapar 41

BRIDES FOR SALE – MS Raghavender 57

SHAME – Mridu Bhandari 61

CITIZENS VS MILITANTS: A BATTLE GONE WRONG – Nagendar Sharma & Neelesh Misra 71

KASHMIR – Nidhi Razdan 81

THREE WEDDINGS AND A FUNERAL – P Sainath 85

GAMBLES OF THE MARKET: FUTILITY OF THE PACKAGES – PK Prakash 89

ECOMONY SLOW GOING – P Vaidyanathan Iyer 95

INNUMERABLE ENCOUNTERS: DOOMED TRIBALS – Punya Prasun Bajpai 109

NIGHT WITHOUT END – Ravik Bhattacharya 117

RAFTING ON THE ROOFTOP OF THE WORLD – Rudraneil Sengupta 127

A TELLTALE NYLON NET AND THE CHANDERPAUL BACKWATERS – Sandeep Dwivedi 137

CUD CHEWING IN THE REALMS OF REALITY – Savita V Harkare 147

RESIDENTS WIN OVER KHAR GYM – Sayli Udas Mankikar 155

FAILED HEALTH SYSTEMS AND UNWARRANTED HYSTERECTOMIES – Shital Morjaria 163

THE CONJUROR OF IMPROBABLE DREAMS – Shoma Chaudhury 171

TOLERATING TOXINS: MERCURY – Sonu Jain 179

WHY THE MEDIA SHOULD WAKE UP THE NEW POLITICAL OLIGARCHY – Sreenivasan Jain 187

AN INCONVENIENT TRUTH FOR SECULAR CPM: NANDIGRAM VICTIMS' MAINLY MUSLIM FACE – Subrata Nagchoudhury 197

LAST CHANCE – Swati Thiyagarajan 205

BUNDELKHAND: MURDER FOR WATER – Umashankar Singh 211

THE 70MM MYTH – Vaishali Sood 219

INDIA'S HIDDEN WARS – VK Shashikumar 225

Foreword

IT is my privilege to introduce to readers the Third Ramnath Goenka Excellence in Journalism Award winners and their award winning entries.

For all the intimations of mortality of journalism that we hear so much of these days, I am delighted that, in the third year of these awards, we received the highest number of entries from the highest number of print and broadcast media organisations.

That is, in itself, a reward for all of us who have a personal and professional stake in the future of the media as we respond to its sweeping changes in technology and customer habits.

In 2006, when the Ramnath Goenka Foundation launched these awards, I had said that if the world's oldest democracy, the United States, has the Pulitzer Prizes for journalism, the world's largest and most diverse democracy has to have its own awards.

To acknowledge excellence is the most powerful way to nurture it. Since some of the best work in journalism is about shining light in dark corners, I hope these awards magnify that light for all of us to see.

More so, when today we have a stream of prophets of doom and gloom.

They are the ones who declare, with full conviction, that the battle has been lost, that user-generated content has marched towards its inevitable triumph. That a cellphone and a camera is all you need to reach to the truth.

This loud ringing of alarm bells drowns many voices. For one, the forces that we think imperil us are some of the same forces that ensure excellence in journalism will never ever be under threat.

You could think of the blogosphere as the biggest army of fact-checkers in the world. Think of the web, its links and hyperlinks, audio and video, as a guarantee that no story can die today. Then, you think of the professional newsroom as a place not just for editing, cutting and pasting but a place where we produce trust. Where the noise gets filtered, enriched with accuracy, credibility, analysis and insight.

All the reporters who have won the awards, illustrate this trust.

Their stories embody it, their subjects demand it. As readers and viewers, we value it. They have shown a commitment to subjects that had they not gone after, would, perhaps, never have been told.

That, in the end, is what excellence in journalism is all about, whatever the technology, whatever the trend, whatever the medium it chooses to take: telling us what we don't know, making us question what we think we know.

Let me quote Rupert Murdoch who has a strange habit of seeing the future in the media before the rest of us: 'Great journalism will always attract readers. The words, pictures and graphics that are the stuff of journalism must feed the mind and move the heart. As long as news organisations create must-read, must-have content, and deliver it in the medium that suits the reader, they will endure.'

The winners of the Third Ramnath Goenka Excellence in Journalism Awards have created must-read, must-have content. We must applaud – because if the future is in their hands, it's pretty safe.

Viveck Goenka
Chairman, The Express Group

Introduction

It is only appropriate that the Ramnath Goenka Excellence in Journalism Awards for are being given in the memory of Ramnath Goenka who founded *The Indian Express*.

Over the years the publications of the Express Group have continuously engaged with political developments and have become known for their strong emphasis on investigative journalism.

Ramnath Goenka first made his mark by confronting the colonial government. Later on in his career he took on entrenched governmental and business interests. While he may have had admirers as well as critics during his lifetime, there is unanimity about his lasting contribution to the way political journalism is conducted in our country.

The Express Group is well respected for its independent editorial positions and rigorous reporting. As a leading player in the print media sector there is also an additional onus of setting a good example for other players. This demonstrative role is important because in recent years the increasing commercialisation of the mass media has also had some adverse effects on journalistic practices.

When media establishments come to be preoccupied with the size of their readership or viewership, there is an increased likelihood of journalists using intrusive news-gathering methods and editors approving of content where facts are often not verified or reported without explaining their proper background.

This tendency of resorting to undue sensationalism or reporting only one side's viewpoint is especially worrying, given the central role of the mass media in a democratic set-up. In many ways the conduct of journalism and politics in a free society is inherently interlinked.

Without the free flow of information and opinions, individuals and groups cannot form the rational choices which are ultimately translated into public policies and governmental action. The essential components of politics – i.e. representation, legislation and administration – all depend on how information is exchanged between the citizens and the government as well as between citizens themselves. Very often, some statements and actions come to gain meaning only on account of the publicity given to them.

At the time of the French Revolution, the press was described as the Fourth Estate in the political establishment. In our times the expanding reach of newspapers, television, radio and the internet – have made the media an even stronger pillar of our political existence. At present, India is one of the few countries where the market for the print media as well as the electronic and digital media has been continuously growing. As more and more Indians become literate and gain access to television and computers, there is also a commensurate responsibility on the news media establishments to present accurate and balanced reports.

The 'freedom of press' is an extension of the fundamental right to 'freedom of speech and expression' provided for under Article 19(1)(a) of the Constitution. In our times, ideas and information reach the masses largely to the extent that they are permitted entry into the prominent dailies and news magazines. With the concentration of the mass media in a few hands, the chances of an idea which is antagonistic to the interests of the proprietors of big newspapers getting access to the market becomes remote. The news media cannot possibly support the public's right to know when there is no acceptance of a duty to inform.

To the press, the public's right to know extends only to what the press elects to tell. There can be no doubt that any mass medium having the greatest circulation would influence the political life of the country because the ideas for which a prominent paper stands have the greatest chance of being circulated among the public. It will affect the economic pattern of the society. The integrity of the news becomes a matter of profound social concern. There is also an affirmative obligation on the part of the government not to abridge the freedom of expression or to allow monopolisation by any party in the mass media. Our vibrant democracy survives to a great extent on the contribution made by the newspapers.

The rights of millions of people who have no scope or opportunity to raise their voice should be given a voice in the mass media. It is said that the victories of freedom of speech must be won in the minds of the people before they are won in the courts. Justice Felix Frankfurter, one of the great American judges, said that at best civil liberties draw only limited strength from legal guarantees and that preoccupation with constitutionality instead of the wisdom of legislative or executive actions is preoccupation with false values. The interface between the news media and the legal system obviously touches on many issues that merit a rigorous discussion.

I hope that The Express Group will continue to engage with these issues while maintaining the high standards of independent and investigative reporting that it is known for.

KG Balakrishnan
Former Chief Justice of India

IS THE LINE BLURRING BETWEEN JOURNALISM AND POLITICS?

PANELISTS

Shobhana Bhartia – Hindustan Times | **Arun Jaitley** – BJP | **Jayanthi Natarajan** – Congress | **Abhishek Manu Singhvi** – Congress | **Rajdeep Sardesai** – CNN-IBN | **P Sainath** – The Hindu
Shekhar Gupta - The Indian Express | **Barkha Dutta** – NDTV | **Sanjay Gupta** – Jagran | **Rajat Sharma** – IndiaTV

Shekhar Gupta: The Ramnath Goenka Memorial media debate is a defining annual debate where we pick up one issue critical to the media. Usually you have media people raising questions of politicians. This time, we have the politicians putting the media on the mat.

Jayathi Natarajan, do you think the line between journalism and politics is blurring?

Jayanthi Natarajan: I feel that politics and journalism are inextricably linked. How we regulate ourselves is something both journalists and politicians have to do together. Earlier, newspaper publishers and newspaper editors kept their distance from the political establishment and never wanted to join it. The political establishment was separate and business was separated. Now, every politician wants to become a businessman and businessmen want to become politicians. So, the lines are blurring.

I want to ask Rajdeep Sardesai: is it not true that business interests have come to stay and the space for pure politics and reporting, has shrunk?

Rajdeep Sardesai: I think we live in times when the intolerance level of politicians has increased manifold. You have politicians who will not appear on television news or will not give interviews unless they are given the questions in advance. They will vet the questions, decide which questions to answer; some will simply not appear on TV because they believe they can get away by never appearing in front of the media. Alongside this growing intolerance of the politician, you have the increasing immorality or the declining morality of the journalist, the proprietor, the publisher and the TV channel owner. But it is basically about moral standards and frankly, I do not blame individual journalists as much as I blame the system.

P Sainath wrote an article recently on `package journalism'. In every state of this country `packages' are being made by newspapers, by news channels which are sold to politicians. You pay per column, centimetre of coverage received or you pay by the amount of time you receive on a channel. Nobody stops it because we are all part of the system.

As in the fields, the higher you go, the more immoral you get. You have editors who network, you have editors who want to become Rajya Sabha MPs, you have editors who do everything but work 24x7. Similarly, some politicians believe that media persons are there to be trampled upon. They know that if you are not willing to ask the questions they want asked, they can find someone else who will.

Thus, the lines are blurring, standards have declined. The corruption that goes on in our profession today should make all of us hang our heads in shame .

Jayanthi Natarajan: Barkha Dutt, would you agree?

Barkha Dutt: I do not disagree with a lot of what Rajdeep has said. But, I think, there is a kind of over-simplistic position-taking. I would not use the word immoral, I would use the word amoral. I think there is a distinction between the two. I am not convinced that as we rise to the top of our hierarchies, there are people who

have sold out to a party, an ideology or that there is a well-defined quid-pro-quo. I do not think it is quite like that. Television enables some sort of distancing between the politician and the journalist. I believe that before the advent of television, all political journalism was source-driven.A lot of journalism is still driven by that but on-the-record journalism actually enables a certain kind of equal access to a story that is afforded to all. I think that has reduced, perhaps even demolished the sort of `clubbyholes' that used to exist in journalism, twenty years ago.

With newspapers you can sometimes tell the slant. With television news it is much more difficult.

Shekhar Gupta: Shobhana Bhartia is it much easier to tell the slant of a newspaper than that of a TV news channel?

Shobhana Bhartia: I think the media as a whole has its head above water in terms of setting the agenda, in terms of exposing political doublespeak, corruption, etc. So, I do not think we can dismiss the media and undermine the role that the media is playing. At an individual level there might be corruption but the truth is that the government is the largest spender and it is the largest advertiser. The kind of arm-twisting that goes on especially in terms of putting pressure on the media at the institutional level is something that is actually blurring the divide between politics and journalism.

Jayanthi Natarajan: P Sainath, should the media not be responsible for regulating itself, why blame the politicians?

P Sainath: When I wrote the story on packages I learned that some of the media `packages' deals simply amounted to extortion. Basically, if you do not take the deal, there will be negative stories.

Shekhar Gupta: This is a case of honour among thieves. You pay me money, I write good things about you; you do not give me money, I go after you.

P Sainath: To address the issue Jayanthi Natarajan raised at the beginning: I do buy the proposition that politics and journalism are inextricably linked. But there is a blurring of distinctions at several levels. Personally, I am far more worried about the blurring of distinctions between journalism and stenography. I see a great deal of what appears in the newspapers and in the news media as stenography which, I believe, is dictated far more by corporate interests than by individual politicians. .

The second blurring of distinctions is between politics and politicians and these are very different things. The news media usually ends up speaking to a specified, certified set of politicians who declare during the elections that there are no issues when there are incredibly important issues unfolding across this country.

The third blurring is between illusion, ideology and imagery. I heard that a very famous newspaper told its staff, 'You will not use the word 'recession' in connection to India because there is no recession in India. Recession is something that is happening in the USA. In India things are looking up, recovery is round the corner.' This is very dangerous politics. And it is very dangerous because you are simplifying an extremely complex situation that is unfolding in the country.

Rajdeep Sardesai: This is true. I think the lines are blurring between political reporting and stenography. 'He said' 'She said' is the basis of most political reporting today particularly on television.

Barkha Dutt: I do not think political stories do not go beyond a certain template because people are not trying or that they do not have access to information. I think it is because we have been seduced by our sources. I cannot tell you how many times you get a call from somebody you know who will say, 'Please remove that particular line from the interview; it will place me in a very embarrassing situation'. Somewhere you know that if you do not remove it, you will not get that interview again.

Rajat Sharma: In my experience, there are people who get into journalism only to get into the Rajya Sabha.

Sanjay Gupta: I always believe in one-way traffic. Once a journalist always a journalist. If you want to cross over, there should be no entry back into journalism.

Abhishek Manu Singhvi: The larger issue is the same everywhere: a conflict of interest. What do we do about a conflict of interest? Nobody minds you wearing multiple hats. This is a world of multiple hats. The point is there is a time and a specific institutionalized mechanism for disclosing those multiple slots and I do not find the disclosure system institutionalized in the print or in the visual media. So my question to you is -- have you thought of that?

I want to give specific example of something that has happened to me often: on a particular TV news discussion programme, the defence policy expert was a member of the defence policy cell of a political party. Nobody disclosed that.

Barkha Dutt: Conflicts of interest related to business holdings can and should be disclosed. But when you talk about individual people – let us say analysts, thinkers - who are associated with political parties, the problem is they have not disclosed themselves in public life, how do you force that? I think everybody has political orientations as individuals. It is the job of an editor to ensure that even the views that you cannot stomach get as much play if they are relevant to the shades of the story.

Rajdeep Sardesai: Partisanship has grown just as intolerance within politics has grown. What I miss as a journalist is the adversarial nature of the relationship that existed. There are politicians today who will not want to be interviewed by a particular journalist or a particular newspaper for a variety of reasons and that is troubling. You are in public life. Once you are in public life, you have got to be open to all forms of scrutiny.

Shobhana Bhartia: This is where the checks and balances you institutionalize need to come in. We have done that in some of our publications. At *Mint* there are checks and balances where you institutionalise the way in which a report comes in. You have crosschecks, you take the other version and it goes for independent evaluation before it actually sees the light of the day . All power does not rest in the hands of just one journalist who may come in with the so-called bias we are discussing.

Rajdeep Sardesai: There is a general fall in standards of journalism and that is the truth.

Shobhana Bhartia: I have a slightly modified view on that. I think the standards have gone up because the competition has forced journalism to acquire a different kind of a profile.

Jayanthi Natarajan: In the vernacular print media, local influences, sometimes, start up a particular kind of propaganda in the media often communal in nature.

Sanjay Gupta: No, I do not think that is true. Maybe, for some small newspapers, not for the larger newspapers;

Rajat Sharma: Well, in Orissa, for example, most of the newspapers are owned by political parties or the sons of political leaders. In Andhra Pradesh, the Chief Minister's son has started a newspaper and a news channel. In Punjab the entire cable network is being controlled by one particular political party.

Shekhar Gupta: Arun Jaitely, do you find that questions you are asked by journalists are politically loaded?

Arun Jaitley: The conventional role of media was that you report what is news on your news pages and you make your editorial comment on your edit page. That is not entering politics. But they have a viewpoint which they try promote and use to influence.

Barkha Dutt: Do you find that you may talk more to people who you believe will be softer on your party line?

Arun Jaitley: I do not think so. I think politicians have started to realise that you have to deal with media of all kinds. You have to use the forum which is provided to you – even on a critical media – to express your viewpoint. My quarrel can never be with the media; my target is the larger audience I want to reach out to and if I can use the media even in a critical debate, I would rather do that.

THE JURY

For The Ramnath Goenka Excellence in Journalism Awards 2007-08, the executive jury comprised some of the most distinguished Indians drawn from various fields:

Dr Bakul H Dholakia, Adviser, Adani Group
Mr Deepak Parekh, Chairman, HDFC
Mr Fali S Nariman, Senior Advocate, Supreme Court of India
Mr Keshub Mahindra, Chairman, Mahindra & Mahindra Ltd
Dr MS Swaminathan, Member of Parliament, Rajya Sabha
Mr Naresh Chandra, Former Cabinet Secretary & Ambassador of India to the United States
Mr NR Narayana Murthy, Founder, Infosys Technologies Ltd
Ms Rama Bijapurkar, Marketing Consultant
Ms Shobhana Bhartia, Chairperson & Editorial Director, HT Media Limited
Mr Shyam Benegal, Film Director
Late Mr Subir Raha, Former Chairman & Managing Director, ONGC

RAMNATH GOENKA
EXCELLENCE IN JOURNALISM AWARDS
2007-08: THE WINNERS

JOURNALIST OF THE YEAR, PRINT
P Sainath, The Hindu

JOURNALIST OF THE YEAR, BROADCAST
Karan Thapar, Infotainment Television

POLITICAL REPORTING, PRINT
Subrata Nagchoudhury & Ravik Bhattacharya, The Indian Express

POLITICAL REPORTING, BROADCAST
Sreenivasan Jain, NDTV

ENVIRONMENTAL REPORTING, PRINT
Sonu Jain, The Indian Express

ENVIRONMENTAL REPORTING, BROADCAST
Swati Thiyagarajan, NDTV

UNCOVERING INDIA INVISIBLE, PRINT
Neelesh Misra & Nagendar Sharma, The Hindustan Times

UNCOVERING INDIA INVISIBLE, BROADCAST
Mridu Bhandari, CNN-IBN

BUSINESS AND ECONOMIC JOURNALISM, PRINT
P Vaidyanathan Iyer, Business World

BUSINESS AND ECONOMIC JOURNALISM, BROADCAST
Abhishek Upadhyay, IBN7

REPORTING ON HIV-AIDS, PRINT
Dnyanesh V Jathar, The Week

REPORTING ON HIV-AIDS, REGIONAL, PRINT
Savita Vikram Harkare, Lokmat

FILMS AND TELEVISION, PRINT
Shoma Chaudhury, Tehelka

FILMS AND TELEVISION, BROADCAST
Vaishali Sood, CNN-IBN

FOREIGN CORRESPONDENT COVERING INDIA, PRINT
Joseph Johnson, Financial Times

SPORTS JOURNALISM, PRINT
Sandeep Dwivedi, The Indian Express

SPORTS JOURNALISM, BROADCAST
Rudraneil Sengupta, CNN-IBN

REGIONAL AWARD, INDIAN LANGUAGE, PRINT
PK Prakash, Madhyamam Daily

REGIONAL AWARD, INDIAN LANGUAGE, BROADCAST
Shital Morjaria, TV9

REGIONAL AWARD, INDIAN LANGUAGE, BROADCAST
MS Raghvender, TV9

REGIONAL AWARD, HINDI, PRINT
Punya Prasun Bajpai, Pratham Pravakta

REGIONAL AWARD, HINDI, BROADCAST
Umashankar Singh, NDTV India

REGIONAL AWARD, NORTHEAST, BROADCAST
VK Shashikumar, CNN-IBN

REGIONAL AWARD, JAMMU AND KASHMIR, PRINT
Muzamil Jaleel, The Indian Express

REGIONAL AWARD, JAMMU AND KASHMIR, BROADCAST
Nidhi Razdan, NDTV

JOURNALISM AWARD FOR BOOKS (NON-FICTION)
Ramachandra Guha *India After Gandhi: The History of the World's Largest Democracy*

PRAKASH KARDALEY MEMORIAL AWARD FOR CIVIC JOURNALISM
Sayli Udas Mankikar, The Hindustan Times

Abhishek Upadhyay

Abhishek Upadhyay, 31, is
Senior Special Correspondent
with IBN7's National Bureau.

A parallel stock market, or the dabba trading, run by brokers flourishes in Mumbai.

DABBA TRADING
Personal Account

While working on this story on dabba trading, a number of times it dawned upon me that searching for something big culminates into certain big changes in your own life. I was then the Gujarat Bureau chief of IBN7 – a job that placed me right in the centre of daily upheavals in terms of gathering news for a 24x7 news channel. Around this time, I came to know that dabba trading was going on in several areas of the state, and that too, right under the nose of the local administration.

This issue concerned hardcore business journalism,. which wasn't my interest area. But as I started getting feedback on this trade and its impact on the economy, my interest in the story grew manifold. The challenge was to take time out of my hectic schedule for this story. Also, professional ethics was a deterrent for the modus operandi required to do the story. I had to make sure that the channel didn't miss any big story from Gujarat and also find time for this new, interesting and rapidly developing story.

To understand dabba trading and the nuances of the racket involved, I got in touch with some people involved in this nefarious business. My source told me that to get to the bottom of the story I would have to pose as a wealthy industrialist while interacting with the dabba traders. Accordingly, we started going to the dabba dens in a hired luxury car. Since I couldn't speak Gujarati, though I could understand the language, I was introduced as a businessman from UP now settled in Ahmedabad.

During this time, my daily schedule used to be really tight, with

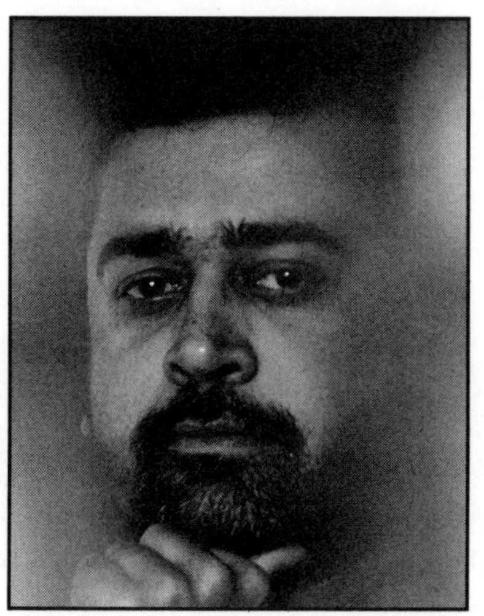

Dnyanesh V Jathar

Dnyanesh V Jathar, 36, is Chief of Bureau with the weekly newsmagazine, *The Week*.

[Most reports concentrate on the problems faced by the commercial sex workers and the trouble in getting treated. But Dnyanesh V Jathar's story focuses on the children who have been orphaned by AIDS.]

AIDS ORPHANS' STORY
Award-Winning Story

Struggles, for some, never cease. When Gauribai lost her son and daughter-in-law to AIDS, she moved into her elder son's house with her orphaned grandchildren. But constant harassment forced them to shift to her ancestral home in Sangli, Maharashtra. 'I had to feed them leftovers thrown to the buffalo,' she said, battling tears. Gauribai was unwell and she had little money to look after the two growing children. So she sent the little girl to her maternal grandmother's house. Her only source of income is her buffalo.

Asit, thirteen, an AIDS orphan, vividly recalls the day he lost his father. 'I was in class four. My mother died ten days later,' he says without emotion. His grandmother Parvati can't control her tears. 'My daughter-in-law, too, was unwell. She died of worry and shock,' she reveals. Asit has a sister three years younger than him. The two children are denied a playful childhood. They are too quiet for their age. But Parvati is glad that the virus has spared her grandchildren.

Parvati's and Gauribai's grandchildren represent a generation of India's HIV-AIDS orphans, who are struggling for survival. There is no official data on the total number of HIV-AIDS orphans in the country. According to the National AIDS Control Organisation, 60,000 children were born with the infection in 2005. According to the Ministry of Health and Family Welfare, 1,67,078 cases of AIDS have been reported from 1986 to 31 March this year. However, the figures given by a senior World Bank official, Aditi Sen, in a 2005 article are staggeringly different. Probably, because as experts say, only 10 per cent of the infected are aware of their status. Sen wrote that the number of children orphaned by AIDS in India is approaching 2 million. The numbers far exceed that of any of the African nations.

An HIV-AIDS orphan is a child who is below eighteen years of age and has lost a parent or both parents to the disease that attacks the person's immune system and makes the person vulnerable to infections. The AIDS orphans are further categorised as 'affected' and 'infected'. In India, the number of infected children is believed to be more than 2.5 lakh.

Meena Seshu, founder of Sangram, an NGO working with AIDS victims, blames the government for the lack of concern. 'In Sangli alone we have 791 HIV orphans on our records. We are just one of the NGOs operating in Sangli,' she says. 'The central and state governments are so obsessed with the larger picture that they are losing touch with harsh realities.'

'HIV and AIDS are brutal escalators of other cruelties that children suffer from,' says Dr P Manorama, founder of Chennai-based Community Health and Education Society (CHES). 'The children are often exploited and abused, increasing their vulnerability to the infection.' The death of their parents almost always leaves them homeless, with the rest of the family ostracising them. Help, if any, comes only from the maternal grandmother. And it is not easy on the already ailing grandparent. Social stigma and lack of proper treatment facilities aggravate the hardship. 'Most grandparents are forced to work in their old age to raise the children. We are providing food and clothing to thirty-two such families in Sangli,' said Meena. Some children also take up huge responsibilities at a very young age to support siblings. But soon, they come face to face with another loss: the death of their grandparents, leaving them orphaned a second time.

All this has a bearing on the emotional and physical well being of the children. 'Whether infected or affected, or orphaned, they have psycho-social needs of their own, which are often neglected,' said Manorama. She recalled incidents of children getting terribly upset when teachers ask them about their parents, who are no more. 'Children need psychological support to deal with death, grief and bereavement, and to face the impact of stigma and discrimination,' she said.

Survival becomes a battle for the children when their HIV-positive mothers are denied ration cards. Even schools shut their gates to these kids. Sometimes financial constraints force children to drop out, despite their desire to study. *The Week* met an affected girl in Maharashtra, who had to leave school after her grandmother fell ill. She has preserved her uniform, hoping to return to school some day.

Ujjwala Lavate, who runs Manavya, a home for HIV-AIDS orphans on the outskirts of Pune, recalled how the villagers harassed kids admitted to the zila parishad school. 'They would throw away the kids' tiffin boxes, pour water on them and even throw stones at them. The teachers remained mute spectators,' she said.

This prompted Ujjwala's mother-in-law, Vijayatai Lavate, who founded Manavya, to start a school in the same compound. Today, it has 53 affected and infected orphans, and receives requests for admission every day. But finding teachers and other staff is tough, admits Ujawala, as 'people avoid coming here because of the stigma'.

The eldest inmate of Manavya is a sixteen-year-old boy, who arrived when he was six. Most of the boys and girls realise the gravity of the infection they were born with. 'They realise they have a short life. Some try to enjoy it to the fullest while some remain angry and despondent,' said Ujjwala. 'I remember one of the boys asking the counsellor why god made him an AIDS orphan when there were so many orphans in the world.' Thirty-seven children at Manavya receive anti-retroviral therapy (ART) that inhibits replication of the virus. Two of them have become resistant to the first line of ART drugs and will soon need second line treatment. 'At present ART is offered at eight centres across the state and we will soon open four more in Kolhapur, Latur, Solapur and Nanded,' said Prakash Sabde, project director of Maharashtra State AIDS Control Society. 'The mother-to-child transmission in the state has come down from 3 per cent to 1 per cent, which is encouraging.'

Delhi-based Naz Foundation has a special home for infected children: at present it has 32 children, the youngest being a two-year old. 'Their nutrition, education, sports and general well-being are taken care of by the home,' said Anjali Gopalan, director of the foundation. 'Besides, we take care of 300 families of affected children. They are given financial support, counselling and medical care.'

There are the few who have a supportive family, who train the children to face life. Eight-year-old Chiranjeev Kalitais is playful like any other kid, the only special thing about him is that he takes anti-retroviral injections. His parents are also HIV-positive. After he was thrown out of kindergarten, the family moved to a new city and put him in a small school where nobody knew about his HIV status. He knew about his illness, its complications and treatment. 'I don't want him to get a shock later on. So I sit with him and watch programmes on AIDS on television to prepare him for the harsh reality,' said his mother.

Children are not the sole victims of the AIDS stigma. Widowed women, who are infected or affected, also face the social fangs of the virus. Saath, an NGO in Latur, Maharashtra, is trying to build a network of HIV-positive women in the district. Its founder, Ziya Saiyed, and her sister Shanoo Shaikh were moved by the cruelties suffered by such women. Shanoo said widowed wives of AIDS patients often plead with doctors to give them a 'negative certificate' so that they and their kids could live with the in-laws. When a baby is born to HIV-positive parents, the family rushes to the doctor to check the baby's status. 'If the child is not infected, the in-laws will accept them or else the mother and child are sent back home,' she said.

In the hinterlands of Maharashtra, we met some HIV-positive women who have kept the truth hidden from the world, so that they and their kids are not ostracised.

The family and relatives torture the orphaned children by throwing them out of the house and grabbing their property. Prashant Bhosale, district coordinator of Sangram, has observed this trend in Sangli as well. 'They don't want the child but their greed does not allow them to part with the child's share of wealth,' he said.

Shunned by all and left alone in the wicked world, the AIDS orphans often fall victim to trafficking and sexual abuse. Three-year-old Sirisha, who lost her parents to AIDS, had a brutal experience. She was picked up by pimps and sexually assaulted. When they found out that her parents had AIDS, they dumped her at Prajwala, a Hyderabad-based NGO.

For Lavanya, her tale of torture was scripted by her mother who sold her for a few hundred rupees to pimps in East Godavari district. Lavanya was raped repeatedly, till a few local people rescued her. When she was brought to Prajwala, her body was bruised and the vagina torn. Eight years old now, Lavanya is alive, thanks to ART drugs.

Dr Sunita Krishnan, founder of Prajwala, said that such children often remain withdrawn and refuse to talk about their problems. 'When some children succumbed to the disease, the other kids inquired about them. We told them they had gone home,' said Sunita. 'So, they felt that if they fell ill they would be taken to hospital and from there sent home. And so, they stopped informing us about their illnesses. We then talked them out of this fear.'

Andhra Pradesh has nearly 5,000 HIV-AIDS orphans; the number of affected children could well be 20 times more. The state has only four orphan care homes, each with 20 beds, and one care and support centre in Hyderabad.

These children need help. Last year, Andhra Pradesh Chief Minister YS Rajasekhar Reddy, announced government's plans to start a home for HIV-AIDS orphans. But it has remained just a plan. In fact, until two years ago, the government was not even willing to admit that affected and infected orphans existed in the state. 'Now they don't deny it blatantly. But still there is no government outfit or policy that looks after these children,' said Sunita. 'The government does not provide any funds to the organisations that look after these children.'

The central govenment, however, is doing its bit to provide better medical care for AIDS patients. The number of government hospitals offering treatment for AIDS patients has increased from 8 in 2004 to 12 today. It is expected to go up to 250 by 2012, as per the National AIDS Control Programme III. Said Father 'Tomy' K, director of Bel-Air Hospital in Panchgani and chairperson of NACP-III's technical resource group on care, support and treatment: 'By 2011, we will be able to provide ART to three lakh patients. But this will not be sufficient as by then the number of positive patients could be much more than the current estimate.'

Most of those who are involved with the cause, however, feel that these children should ideally grow up with their families in their villages. 'There is a remarkable difference in a child brought up within his family's support structure and those brought up in institutions,' said Meena. 'Those who grow up in families can cope with the world whereas an institution is a protected atmosphere. In community care a child develops more skills, enabling him to lead a more successful life. And, can we ever have enough institutions to accommodate and care for all HIV orphans in India?' Sunita, too, feels that 'uprooting children and putting them in an institution is not an ideal situation.' Fr Tomy feels that the extended families of the orphans should be strengthened by providing them financial and technical help.

M Muthupandian, who manages CHES's HIV-AIDS Orphans' Ashram in Chennai, said they always tried to take the children back to their immediate family or friends. Said Unicef project officer Dr Devashish Dutta: 'Orphanages should be the last resort for AIDS orphans. The interests of the child are best served when they grow up in a family environment. The best way is to normalise them.'

The safety and comfort of the family is best, echo all, but are the families listening? Today, over two million affected children live in community homes run by NGOs, or railway platforms, or wander the streets, or are abandoned at village fairs. They represent a generation of 'lost souls' in a so-called upwardly mobile India.

As the nation enters the third and crucial stage of the NACP, it needs a comprehensive child policy that looks at HIV-AIDS, its dangerous ramifications and issues of care and protection of the orphans. The government should wake up to the reality, and act, said the experts, calling for a separate Children's Bill. 'We have been lacking in adequate response but NACP-III has dealt with the issue of orphans in great detail,' said Fr Tomy. 'As a document, it is flawless. What remains to be seen is how much can you implement. NACO is even thinking of constituting a separate technical resource group to deal with the issue of HIV orphans and vulnerable children.'

The experts recommend that actions taken should be guided by four strategic insights:

1. The need for urgency as the problem is not tomorrow's but today's, increasing every minute

2. A sense of realism that recognises community-based responses as not only the most desirable alternative, but also as the

economically feasible alternative to provide the coverage needed

3. The need to go to scale at once with taluk-level care initiatives.

4. The need for all key stakeholders to assume the most appropriate and cost-effective roles possible, such as integration of programmes for children affected by AIDS in all departments dealing with children and starting an equal private-public partnership.

(Some names have been changed to protect identity.)

Personal Account

I clearly remember that meeting with Prakash Kardaley, then resident editor of *The Indian Express's* Pune edition. I was a rookie reporter, among the juniors in the team, having been there a little over a year. Master, as Mr Kardaley was affectionately referred to, summoned me to his cabin. A summon to Master's cabin could be the highest or lowest point in the life of a reporter, depending on whether he had filed a good story or had had a miserable miss. I prepared myself for the worst and entered his cabin. 'Would you like to work in the Kolhapur bureau?' Master asked. I was excited but did not show it. It had been a dream to work in a moffusil bureau. The selfish thought behind this was the simple fact that most of the stories filed by a city team reporter in Pune went into the city-centric *Newsline* supplement and thus had limited readership. Reports from the districts appeared – depending on the importance of the story – in the state or nation pages, ensuring a wider reach.

Having agreed to take up the offer, I was dispatched for a recce trip to Kolhapur and south Maharashtra, the regions I would have to cover. Having been born in the neighboring district of Sangli, I had emotional ties with these districts. It was during this trip that I first met senior journalist Vasant Bhosale (now resident editor of Sakal in Kolhapur) and his wife Meena Seshu, who runs Sangram, an NGO for HIV-AIDS affected people.

I was happy with my Kolhapur assignment. I travelled frequently to the interiors of Kolhapur and to neighbouring districts like Sangli and Satara, nosing out interesting stories. The then collectors of Kolhapur and Sangli – Arvind Singh and Dr

Nitin Kareer, respectively – were always welcoming. During one such visit to Sangli, Dr Kareer informed me about his ambitious campaign to create awareness about AIDS. After that meeting, if I remember correctly, I went to attend a function organised by Sangram, where I saw a number of children whose parents were affected by AIDS. On another trip to Sangli, I also visited a centre of AIDS orphans run by Bhagini Nivedita, an institution founded by Kusumtai Ghanekar (she died recently), my mother's childhood acquaintance. Back then in 1998-99, little did I know that these children would be the focus of my story nine years later, in 2007.

In May 1999, I joined *The Week*. One of the best things about my job here is that the editors and the management are always encouraging when it comes to reporting stories on social issues from rural hinterlands. I got to do many stories on social issues which made an impact like malnutrition of children in Melghat and Nandurbar, farmers' suicides and violence against de-notified tribes like killings of Fasse Pardhis in Marathwada region.

I was also invited to be a member of a fact-finding team that presented its report on killing of a Fasse Pardhi family in Osmanabad district to State Human Rights Commission. Another story, on Sindhutai Sapkal, a social worker working for orphan and destitute children, won her a prestigious award in Punjab. My story on Dr Baba Adhav, who was The Week's Man of The Year in 2007, led to a decision by then railway minister, Lalu Prasad Yadav to regularise the employment of railway porters across the country. Dr Adhav, who works for these porters and other such unorganised labourers, wrote to *The Week*'s editors stating that Mr Yadav happened to read the story and this eventually led to his decision to regularise porters in the grade of pointsman in railway service.

HIV-AIDS came back to haunt me when Shiv Sena legislator Dr Neelam Gorhe told me a very disturbing complaint that her NGO, Stree Aadhar Kendra, had received from Nandurbar district. It was a case in which a woman had alleged that her husband, an Ayurvedic doctor, had used an infected syringe on her and their newborn daughter, and had abandoned them. I could not believe it at first. So I checked with the superintendent of police of Nandurbar. He said that a complaint was indeed filed at a local police station and the medical tests of the woman confirmed her

HIV positive status. I filed the story after speaking to doctors and experts at National AIDS Research Institute.

I feel that lifestyle induced health issues are taking precedence over core health issues that our nation faces. The media attention these days is more focussed on glamorous lifestyle diseases. Malnutrition, TB, malaria are not as important despite the fact that they kill people in equally large numbers, if not more. Public healthcare or the lack of it, has always been very close to my heart as a subject. Thus my reading of health issues has been more public-health centric and health-policy centric. It was during one such reading sessions that I came across a report by Aditi Sen, a World Bank official, on a website which estimated that there are nearly two million HIV-AIDS orphans in India. Twenty lakh is a mind-boggling number, even in a nation of over 100 crore. I felt overwhelmed. In a day or two after having read this I spoke to Meenatai Seshu to check if the statistics – two million – could be true. She told me that she could not confirm it but said that it cannot be ruled out either as in Sangli alone there were over 600 registered AIDS orphans in Sangram's records. I submitted a story outline to the editors quoting the report and my conversation with Meenatai. I also requested that my colleagues from other bureaus send me inputs for the story. The story was approved without any delay and I was asked to anchor it.

As our senior photographer Janak Bhat and I began work on the story, we travelled to Pune, Sangli, Tasgaon, Latur, Ausa and Mahabaleshwar to meet orphans and their relatives, NGOs, and experts. In Pune, I met Mrs Ujjwala Lavate who runs Manavya, a home for AIDS orphans. During our interaction she told me that she receives at least four phone calls every day. 'In earlier times, people abandoned leprosy patients, that is what they do with HIV-AIDS orphans now.' She told me how she often faced shortage of staff. 'We don't get staff, doctors, even drivers for that matter. People just want to stay away. Touring Sangli and its interiors like Tasgaon, Palus with Meenatai's colleagues from Sangram was an eyeopener. Here I met an elderly woman who was living with her grandson infected with AIDS. '*Sunbai Geli, Mulga Gela, He Valvan Darapudhe Theun Gela. Kadhikadhi Sonarane Mhashila taklela Anna Khayla Ghalun Natvana Vadhavtey Mi* (Son died, daughter-in-law died, they left him behind. On some occasions I have fed him food that a goldsmith had left behind for a buffalo),' she said in Marathi. As she spoke, tears began rolling down her cheeks. She spoke for nearly half an hour and I listened in rapt attention. A point came when I felt I just could not listen to her any more. She explained how her elder son's wife first began harassing her and her grandson. When she could not suffer it any longer, she decided to live separately. 'I left that house and began living in an old broken house which my husband had left behind.' The grandmother had shaken me to the core. As I rose to leave, I felt a vacuum growing within, tears welled up in my eyes. If the orphans in Pune were living in a shelter run by an NGO, in Sangli, they were living with their grandparents who were mostly in their seventies. Some were forced to work in order to look after their grandchildren. They cried very often, blamed relatives but they had not given up hope. In Latur, Ziya Shaikh and her sister Shanu offered me another glimpse of how familial politics determines the fate of children born to HIV-AIDS affected parents. 'If the newborn is a boy, he is sent immediately to the testing centre to ascertain whether he is HIV infected or not. If the baby tests negative the in-laws of the woman take him to their home, if he tests positive, both the mother and the baby are sent back to her maternal house,' they said. While I was travelling in Maharashtra, my colleagues, N Bhanutej (Bangalore), Lalita Iyer (Hyderabad), Payal Saxena (New Delhi) and Srinivasa Ramanujam (Chennai) were meeting the affected and infected orphans and their caretakers in their respective states. Lalita put me on to her friend Sunita Krishnan, who runs an organisation, Prajwala. Sunita helped me immensely in understanding the issues in Andhra Pradesh and how on the government's part there is intent, but not much action, as it often happens. 'Children are, by and large, neglected. Among them HIV-AIDS orphans – both infected and affected – would be the last in the line. We need a policy not just for AIDS orphans but a comprehensive national plan for children that highlights their vulnerabilities. In this country we need to create a mandate for children,' she spoke firmly. Like Sunita, Dr P Manorama of CHES from Chennai, gave me a clear picture about Tamil Nadu. She actually helped me put together a policy draft of sorts that unfortunately could not be published for want of space.

I used to think that the line of difference between sympathy and empathy is thin. As I worked on the story, it became thicker. I always thought journalists were strong on the empathy quotient. However, I think I understood what empathy really means while working on this story. If a few days of interaction with AIDS orphans could move me to tears, what must have been the emotional state of grandparents when their children succumbed to AIDS, leaving behind helpless children. What kind of societal pressure and opposition activists like Meenatai, Mrs Lavate, Sunita or Dr Manorama may have faced when they started their work.

What does it take to nurse a hope when the reality is so stark and grim, what keeps these grandparents going, why don't these mothers get ration cards easily, why can't state transport corporations give a free travel pass to these children and their grandparents so that they can travel to district hospitals for regular checkups, why don't these kids and their families get enough government support – so many questions kept crowding my mind.

All these questions are resurfacing as I write this article. After I won the award, I called Meenatai to inform her and thank her for helping me. 'Dnyanesh, journalists win awards but what about my children, what about their daily struggle?' she asked calmly. My elation fizzled out as her words penetrated my thoughts. Her question haunts me, I have no answers.

Joseph Johnson

Joseph Johnson, 38, was a former Foreign Correspondent, covering India for the *Financial Times*. He is now a Conservative Party MP.

[Coming in the wake of Sachar Committee report. Joseph Johnson's story locates the Indian Muslim in his complex environment – riots, terrorism, poverty and occasional stardom.]

RADICAL THINKING

Award-winning Story

Shortly before 8 a.m. on 27 February 2002, a fire broke out on the Sabarmati Express as it pulled out of Godhra, a town prone to religious violence in the Indian state of Gujarat. Many of the passengers were Hindu pilgrims returning from a ceremony called Chetavani Yatra. Rescuers pulled 58 bodies out of carriage S-6, all of them charred beyond recognition. An official report, published four years later, in 2006, concluded that the blaze had been an accident, but at the time it was blamed on Muslim youths, who were accused of throwing petrol-bombs at the saffron-clad pilgrims.

The blood-letting started the next morning and continued until early May, leaving about 2,500 Muslims murdered. Armed with knives, fire bombs and sharpened ceremonial tridents, and guided by electoral rolls that revealed the location of Muslim homes, mobs began to move across the state. 'What ensued was a ghastly sight the like of which, since bleeding partition days, no Indian eye had seen,' wrote Justice VR Krishna Iyer, in a report by the Tribunal of Concerned Citizens, an independent body composed mostly of retired judges.

The first to suffer were the largely middle-class inhabitants of a housing complex called the Gulberg Society in the Chamanpura district of central Ahmedabad. The centre of an Indian commercial city saw a medieval and macabre dance of death, humiliation and revenge, reported the Tribunal in its account of the pogrom, Crime Against Humanity, which was based on 2,094 statements taken from the survivors.

By 10 a.m., a mob of between 20,000 and 25,000 people had

surrounded the Gulberg Society, where many had fled to take shelter in the home of Ahsan Jafri, an influential trade unionist and former MP from the Congress party. In his desperation, Jafri made over 200 calls for help that day. During earlier bouts of violence in Ahmedabad, he had been able to protect his community, but not this time. At 2.30 p.m., the politician was dragged out of his house, slashed with swords until his limbs were severed, and then set alight. Around 70 others from the Gulberg Society died with him that day.

A series of investigations by the Tribunal of Concerned Citizens, by India's National Human Rights Commission and by Human Rights Watch in New York later accused two Hindu extremist groups, the Vishwa Hindu Parishad and its youth wing, the Bajrang Dal, of masterminding the massacres. Numerous human rights groups, including Human Rights Watch (HRW), argued that the state government, led by Narendra Modi, a senior figure in the Hindu nationalist Bharatiya Janata Party (BJP), had been wilfully deficient in its response.

'It was the first full-blooded pogrom in India's independent history,' says Ashutosh Varshney, a professor of political science at the University of Michigan. 'It was driven by hatred and ideologically charged.'

Modi's approach to the riots may have helped him solidify his electoral base ahead of that year's state elections. 'For every action, there is an equal and opposite reaction,' he said. The machinery of justice, to the extent it was used at all, was stacked against Muslims, who accounted, perversely, for the vast majority of those arrested. HRW alleged that the government of Gujarat had systematically obstructed efforts to bring the perpetrators to justice.

Police refused to file reports for the missing, let alone arrest suspects. Witnesses who came forward to identify attackers were harassed, threatened or bribed into turning hostile on the witness stand, or simply into not showing up when the case went to trial. Only Muslims who withdrew their testimony were allowed to return to their neighbourhoods. For four years, impunity prevailed. Only in early 2006, following the exasperated intervention of the Supreme Court in New Delhi, was there some token progress, with the conviction, by a Mumbai court, of nine people for the murder of fourteen Muslims who had taken refuge in a bakery.

According to many human rights groups, the state government was lukewarm in its response to the Gujarat riots of 2002.

'Gujarat was a turning point,' says Sayeed Khan, who runs Muslim Youth of India, a Mumbai-based group that is battling against the radicalisation of the country's young Muslims. 'After Gujarat, young Muslims started asking themselves: "Why are they killing us just for being Muslims?"... All over India, there are youths who think there should be revenge. And they're ready to do whatever it takes.'

In the past eighteen months, India has been lashed by a wave of terror attacks outside the disputed state of Jammu and Kashmir, the main battleground for Islamic militants waging a jihad against Indian 'occupation'. It started in October 2005, on the eve of the Hindu holiday of Diwali and the Muslim festival of Eid, when bombs exploded in markets across Delhi, killing 62 and injuring 210. It continued in March 2006, when blasts in Varanasi, a city holy to Hindus, killed 15 and injured 60.

The following month, explosions at Delhi's main mosque, the Jama Masjid, injured 13. Thirty-five Kashmiri Hindu villagers were shot dead in May. Then, on 11 July, a date that has become known as India's 9/11, terror struck Mumbai, with seven bombs hitting the commuter train network, the backbone of the city's transport system, killing 209 and injuring more than 700. In

Terrorism mainly springs from radicalised elements within the system and external support fans the dissatisfaction.

September, blasts in Malegaon, a town in Maharashtra, prone to communal violence, killed 37 Muslims as they left a mosque after Friday prayers.

And then on 18 February this year, as the five-year anniversary of the Godhra train attack approached, terrorists placed kerosene bombs linked to sophisticated timers on an overnight train from Delhi to the Pakistani city of Lahore. Six minutes before midnight, as the Samjhauta Express travelled through late-winter wheat fields north-west of Delhi, two firebombs exploded inside denim-clad briefcases, causing an inferno in carriages packed with slumbering passengers that left 69 dead.

The catalogue of atrocities demands explanation. Why is India, a country that prides itself on its democratic safety valves and vibrant political system, proving so vulnerable to terrorism? Indian authorities have in almost every instance laid the blame on Pakistan-based militant groups, Ajai Shukla, a leading security affairs analyst in New Delhi, says India is looking for scapegoats beyond its borders.

'While external support certainly fans the flames of disaffection, terrorism increasingly springs from radicalised elements within India that have not been able to address issues by other means,' says Shukla. 'Besides the disaffection in India's north-eastern states and in Kashmir, Gujarat is now becoming a fertile recruiting ground for terrorist cells.'

This tendency to blame the 'foreign hand' also ignores the assessment that even sophisticated Pakistan-based militant groups are likely to be dependent on local terror cells to carry out their attacks. 'After the Mumbai blasts, there is now no doubt that there are terror cells in India,' says Varshney. 'That kind of attack cannot be undertaken without a deep local knowledge of Mumbai and without serious local cooperation, whether paid for or ideologically motivated.'

Academics believe the roots of India's worsening terrorism problem can be found in a complex fusion of greed and grievance. While an unscrupulous criminal underworld plays an important role in facilitating and carrying out terror attacks, that is just part of the story. Despite three years of turbo-charged growth, there are still hundreds of millions living in abject poverty. Some, inevitably, succumb to the blandishments of recruiters from the country's myriad insurgencies and extremist movements.

The successful integration of India's Muslim population has strategic significance for the subcontinent and for the political West. The Muslim community forms the second largest religious group in the country and represents just under 14 per cent of the 1.1 billion population.

In global terms, India has the largest Muslim population after Indonesia and Pakistan. By the time its population stabilises, sometime in the middle of this century, demographers expect it to number between 320 and 340 million, and its share of the total population, by then to be almost 19 per cent. India's success as a society will, to a considerable extent, depend on it reversing a worrying trend towards radicalisation in certain sections of that population.

Many take this for granted. George W Bush, for example, repeatedly hailed India as a model for the successful integration of a large Muslim population in a secular political framework. However, such complacency should have been punctured following the government's release of a shocking study of how the country's Muslims as a whole have fared since independence.

Commissioned by the prime minister and produced by a committee chaired by Rajinder Sachar, a former justice of the Delhi

High Court, the report presents a sharp counterpoint to perceptions of India as a stable, inclusive and multicultural society. Of all the groups yet to benefit from India's spectacular recent growth – set to hit 9.2 per cent this year – none, apart from so-called dalits (once known as 'untouchables') and tribals, have fared as poorly as Muslims.

'Muslims in India have this sense of being degraded,' says Sarfaraz Arzu, editor and publisher of the *Hindustan Daily*, Mumbai's oldest Urdu-language newspaper. 'They're not getting their share of the national pie. They are not the only section of society untouched by this growth, but they are excluded because of their identification as a distinct religious group, which means, in simple terms, that they're targeted for what they are.'

India's 140 million Muslims are divided along class, caste and sectarian lines, with sociologists describing their relationship to the rest of Indian society as one of 'upper class inclusion and mass exclusion'. A small elite – typified by the Khans that rule Bollywood, the aristocratic Nawabs and businessmen such as Azim Premji, chairman of Wipro, a leading software group – thrives in the new India, while the masses, mostly low-caste converts from Hinduism, face marginalisation.

Sachar notes that many Muslims are unable to buy or rent property in the area of their choice and find their children rejected from good schools. This has contributed to the sharp growth in the number of madrassas. The phenomenon should not be exaggerated: just 4 per cent of Muslim school-age children now attend full-time madrassas, according to Sachar. But in some states, including the populous northern state of UP, where more than 7 per cent of Muslim schoolchildren are being educated in religious seminaries, madrassas are spreading rapidly.

Behind the green gates of 41 Mohammed Ali Road is the Minara Masjid complex, where 450 young Muslim men aged between twelve and twenty-five live and study at the madrassa attached to the mosque. 'There has been a 100 per cent increase in the number of madrassas in India over the last five years,' says Syed Ather Ali, principal of the madrassa, which provides students with lodging, board, books and medical care. Students pass their days translating and memorising the Koran and their nights sleeping on mats in a number of concrete-floored dormitories.

The education system is failing India's Muslims, whose average literacy level was 59.1 per cent in the 2001 census, compared with a national average of 65 per cent. Just 4 per cent of Muslims above the age of twenty are graduates or diploma holders, compared to 7.4 per cent for the country as a whole. Muslims, tellingly, account for 1.3 per cent of students at the elite Indian Institutes of Management.

Poorly educated Muslims generally end up working as self-employed, economically vulnerable casual labour. Those Muslims who do receive regular salaries tend to occupy the lowest rungs within organisations. The proportion of Muslims living below the poverty line, at 31 per cent, is higher than the 22.7 per cent for the country as a whole.

Sachar found that Muslims had an 'abysmally low' share of prized government jobs, accounting for just 3 per cent of posts in the Indian Administrative Service, the elite corps of the civil bureaucracy, 1.8 per cent of the Indian Foreign Service and 4 per cent of the police. They had such a low profile in the military that the Ministry of Defence denied Sachar the data. The community is only consistently over-represented in the prison population. In Maharashtra, for example, Muslims account for more than 40 per cent of those jailed for less than a year.

'The root problem is economic,' says MJ Akbar, editor the *Asian Age*. 'If you look at Indian Muslims, their traditional businesses, such as crafts and weaving, have been wiped off the economic map, and there has been no effort to create jobs in the space stolen from them. And now the malls that are coming up across the country are about to eliminate their traditional role as suppliers of meat, wiping out another large source of employment. The impact of all of this will be ten years of serious violence.'

The potential for such violence is a terrifying underlying reality. Communal violence left 40,000 dead and injured between 1950 and 1995, according to research by academics Steven Wilkinson and Ashutosh Varshney. The costs of riots have been overwhelmingly borne by Muslims, forced to leave their homes, businesses and land for sanctuary in safe Muslim areas.

Sofia Khan, a forty-two-year-old human rights activist, moved to Juhapura, a Muslim ghetto in Ahmedabad, in the aftermath of the July 2006 Mumbai commuter train attacks. She says she was hounded out of her home after local television stations advised viewers to check out their neighbours. 'If you talk to the minority community today, they're just pushed into a corner. For us, there's no "Vibrant Gujarat" (Modi's slogan for the state), it's just v iolent Gujarat.

'It's five years now and there's no sense of remorse in society at large, no sense of justice. Overwhelming feelings of insecurity and fear, these are our biggest problems. Fear that you will be targeted, fear that you will be victimised, fear that there will be another backlash. You cannot open your mouth. You cannot engage in human rights activities. Many people who were engaged in relief work are now in prison.'

Juhapura is the biggest ghetto in Gujarat, with a population of 400,000, that increases with every communal riot in the state. 'It's just as if it was a border between India and Pakistan,' Khan says.

From her fourth-floor office, the trained lawyer overlooks a relief camp for victims of the 2002 riots. NGOs say as many as 35,000 remain camped in 81 semi-permanent colonies set up by Islamic relief organisations. Access to public services is poor. India is in the throes of a telecom revolution, but Khan's building in Juhapura cannot get the state-controlled service provider to install a landline: 'There is not a single bank or broadband internet connection in the area and you can forget about having a public park or a library, those are luxuries.'

When religious organisations such as the Islamic Relief Committee, Jamaat Ulema-e-Hind and Imarat-e-Shariya opened madrassas, they filled a vacuum left by the state.

'The government has not done anything for us,' says Mukti P, a middle-aged woman carrying water pots. 'Whatever has been done for us has been done by our own people.' Abeda P, thirty-six, whose husband and daughter died as they hid in Jafri's house, says: 'When Narendra Modi dies, then there will be communal harmony in Gujarat because (alive) he will not allow it in the state.'

Ravi Nair, a human rights activist who runs the South Asian Human Rights Documentation Centre, says these relief camps provide 'cannon fodder for Islamic fundamentalist groups'. His assessment finds an echo with Father Cedric Prakash, a Jesuit priest, who was recently honoured by the French government for his work promoting religious harmony in Ahmedabad. 'The whole ghetto is on the boil,' he warns.

'We're pushing an entire community to the brink. Forgiveness and reconciliation can only happen in the context of justice. Suppose my daughter's been raped, my only son's been killed, and I can see the person responsible behaving with impunity. How then do I bring myself to forgive?'

That day, Modi and I sit down together. The apostle of Hindutva ('Hinduness') has just addressed investors at the 'Vibrant Gujarat' conference in Gandhinagar. He is an electrifying orator, and the global business community cannot get enough of a man in charge of a state that expanded by more than 11 per cent last year, making it the fastest growing investment hotspot in India.

For the moment, though, he remains something of a pariah within the Indian political system, a status that has been reinforced by the fact that he has been banned from travelling to the US. In March 2005, the US State Department publicly denied him a visa, pointing in a statement to a section of the Immigration and Nationality Act barring entry to any foreign government official who 'was responsible for or directly carried out, at any time, particularly severe violations of religious freedom'.

Modi wants to talk business, not religious politics. Amid increasingly fierce competition between Indian states for investment, he has adopted the most can-do attitude of all chief ministers. Across the country, the government's policy of promoting Special Economic Zones (SEZs), Chinese-style capitalist enclaves, has run into fierce opposition and many chief ministers have gone off the idea. But not Modi: 'The whole of Gujarat is a SEZ,' he says. 'S stands for spirituality, E for entrepreneurialism, and Z for zeal.'

Would he like the US to lift the travel ban? 'It is up to them,' he says without hint of rancour. Asked why Gujarati Muslims feel marginalised and excluded from this growth, he shakes his head as if to imply a logical impossibility. 'This state has constant double-digit growth. Would that be possible if 10 per cent of the population were excluded? That's my question to the questioners.'

The glib response saddens Rahul Dholakia, the director of *Parzania*, a film about the Gujarat pogrom that is essential viewing for anyone wanting to understand why the events of 2002 continue to have such a far-reaching impact on the politics of religious identity in India. Based on the true story of a father and mother's tragic hunt for their cricket-loving son, Azhar Mody, who was swept up by the sword-wielding mob that ransacked the Gulberg Society, it is, at times, just too painful to watch.

Parzania has received critical acclaim but the Bajrang Dal, the Hindu extremist youth group, has seen to it that no cinema in Ahmedabad, Gandhi's adoptive town, has yet dared show it.

Sixty years ago, on the eve of Independence, Nehru, called on his countrymen to help him 'build the noble mansion of free India where all her children may dwell'. He declared: 'We are citizens of a great country on the verge of bold advance, and we have to live up to that high standard. All of us, to whatever religion we may belong, are equally the children of India with equal rights, privileges and obligations. We cannot encourage communalism or narrow-mindedness, for no nation can be great whose people are narrow in thought or in action.'

His words are as true today as they were then.

Karan Thapar

Karan Thapar, 54, is President, Infotainment Television and makes programmes for CNN-IBN and CNBC TV18. He is a well-known TV anchor and interviewer.

'My objective is to make people in power accountable,' says Karan Thapar, Journalist of the Year.

A CRITIQUE OF TELEVISION NEWS
Personal Account

I want to write about what I still insist on calling a recent 'miracle' of the Indian media landscape as well as its limitations – the explosion of news on television. Just over a decade ago TV news was a government monopoly. We were all captive audiences of Doordarshan. Today there are more than 60 dedicated news channels whilst several others have news bulletins in their daily schedules. And I haven't included BBC, CNN, Bloomberg and Channel NewsAsia in this reckoning. They would be there regardless of the Indian news miracle.

As a result, it's not an exaggeration to claim that news on television is a popular programme. Even if the viewership at any one time does not suggest that two other factors do: the enthusiasm of broadcasters for news and the willingness of advertisers to support it.

One consequence of this is that we as a nation are better informed or, at least, we have the potential to be. I accept that it all depends on what you watch. But the very profusion of news and its easy accessibility raise questions we would not have asked before. Some of these questions might seem heretical coming from a television news producer. Others point towards debates and solutions the West has encountered but which we in India are yet to experience. But in either case, they are questions that need to be asked. I want to raise some of them here and suggest hesitant answers.

Let me start by asking what sort of news do we get from television? It's pretty much immediate – we no longer have to wait for tomorrow's papers to find out what's happened today. Television news channels can tell you within a minute. Some boast of doing so even faster. It can also be visual and highly illustrative. Television shows rather than describes. You feel as if you are there witnessing for yourself. Although I do not wish to exaggerate the point, in that sense it can be participatory.

But television news has two important limitations and beyond that an inherent tendency to sensationalise. Let's tackle the latter first. The screen shows only what the camera films. In turn the camera films only what the cameraman focuses upon. This is not merely a question of subjective choice – although it is that too – it is also a technical matter. The camera will film the visual it focuses on excluding whatever is on either side of it. You do not get the picture the eye can see. You only get what the lens can fit in. Thus a succession of close ups of a fire or of dead bodies or of fallen trees could suggest an enormous blaze or a massacre or severe cyclonic destruction. That may be the case but it's also possible that it may not. Yet, in either event the mind of the viewer will leap to this conclusion. The danger is it could be the wrong one.

This is what I call television's inherent tendency to sensationalise. This is also why the statement, 'It has to be true because I saw it on the box,' is actually misleading or, at least, based on a fallacious understanding of television. But this problem is easily taken care of – either by pulling out and showing wide shots that put events in perspective or by wisely written commentary. The only thing is when journalists are up against tight time deadlines – which is more often than not the case – such balancing can be squeezed out.

The two limitations of television news are more difficult to tackle and in India, at least, I have so far seen little attempt to tackle them. At times there is even little acknowledgement of them.

The first limitation is that TV has problems handling what it cannot show. An anchor's talking head is not easy to follow – aural information is the most difficult to comprehend, particularly when it is detailed – and graphics or photographs don't always help. This is why news bulletins occasionally ignore what they cannot film. In a Western democracy – where the reach of TV cameras is enormous – this has minimal impact. In India – where the reach of TV cameras is comparatively minimal – the impact can be enormous.

This is why there is so much more news in the papers than on television. This is why we 'hear' or 'read' about events like the ABVP (Akhil Bharatiya Vidyarthi Parishad) banning jeans in Lucknow colleges but never see it. After all how do you show a ban? More importantly this is also why the budget is so boring on television. First, it's just a speech but then there's the question what is the speech about. That's an even bigger problem. What it's about is not the price of commodities, not even the tax on the price of commodities, but the change in the tax on the price of commodities and sometimes the percentage change in that tax. None of that is easy to visualise so, instead, we are shown potatoes and tomatoes. No wonder those who follow the budget on screen usually doze off.

The second limitation of television news is more serious. It has, to quote a phrase made famous in Britain by John Birt in the 1970s, a bias against understanding. To explain that, I'll use a contentious desi example.

When television tells you about a gruesome event like the murder of Graham Staines it brings home the horror of what happened as no other medium can. It sickens you. It tugs at your emotions. It stabs at your conscience. And all of that is very welcome.

But what television does not do is to explain why this happened. I don't mean who did it, how, where, when and at what time. Those facts are easily communicated. I mean why? How could followers of one of the world's most peaceful religions turn upon a single man and his two children? How could we – a people who think of ourselves as tolerant, welcoming, loving – kill so ruthlessly and mercilessly?

These are questions of context, of background, of history. In the Graham Staines case they were answered – if at all they were – by a judicial commission. No doubt newspapers don't tackle them adequately either – although in the op-ed pages they try – but then newspapers don't make the same impact when they report such tragedies. Television does. Worse that impact pushes people towards easy conclusions. A rush to judgement follows.

Two consequences stand out: we all think we know the truth behind Graham Staines' grisly death and the guilty party – if I can use that emotive term – feels hard done by. But the truth is embedded in a context television news does not and did not explore and, therefore, most of us have not found out about. And the guilty party may well be guilty but we have not as yet fully established its guilt nor, more importantly, understood it.

Inadequate appreciation of the limitations of television and its inherent tendency to sensationalise, coupled with the fact that news on television is both more frequent and accessible and often has greater impact, can lead to unintended distortions or imperfect understanding. In such circumstances news and views can become perilously mixed up.

So what's the solution? I promised hesitant answers and, hesitantly, I shall attempt them.

The first lesson is that reportage is not enough. We need more context, more explanation, more background. In turn that means we need more specialist correspondents – more correspondents with dedicated fields to furrow – and fewer fire-fighters. It also means that for most important developments television news needs to supplement reports of what's happened with analysis of why and what it means. In other words, news analysis has to become part of news reportage.

The second lesson is that we need more current affairs. News on its own is not enough. We need programmes that go deeper, wider, further. I know that in India, at least in theory, we have them but they fail to serve their purpose. I include my own in that judgement unreservedly. Such programmes work when they take their subject more seriously than the personalities participating in them. In India, it's the other way around. We need the cold analysis of current affairs. Instead we have the spectacle and tamasha of clashing viewpoints. We need to shed light but end up generating heat.

Finally, television needs the sort of wisdom that comes with age. It has in plenty enthusiasm, dedication, tireless striving, and ceaseless vigil. All of that is remarkable in an industry so young. Let that not be gainsaid. But it does not have the capacity to reflect, to pronounce wisely, to be sagacious, to speak with gravitas. No doubt such qualities are difficult to acquire but their absence is telling.

Of course there's a lot more that can and should be done but my intention is to raise questions, focus attention and, hopefully, start a debate. For that purpose, I think, I have written enough.

MS Raghavender

MS Raghavender, 34, is Senior Producer, TV9, Karnataka.

[Women are being sold off in Marwar, Rajasthan, where the sex ratio is very low. It is done in the guise of marriage. The only difference is that here, the fathers know their daughters are going into flesh trade.]

BRIDES FOR SALE

Personal Account

The story narrated by the girl had been haunting me for some time. I think I would never have been aware of the social evil that dumbfounded me, had I not visited the jail. It was there the unfortunate girl had told me about female trafficking.

Belonging to a decent poor family in north Karnataka, she lost her father, the sole breadwinner, when she was only ten years old. After the father's death her mother decided to marry her off as soon as she reached puberty. They also started looking for a suitable groom for her but unfortunately, all their efforts went in vain because of the demand for dowry. The mother kept on worrying about her daughter's marriage. However, one fine day, their prayers were answered. A man came in search of a bride. He was handsome, did not demand any dowry, and was also ready to take care of all the marriage expenses. Reportedly a rich person, he did not speak Kannada, the local language – he was from Rajasthan. Still, the mother was very pleased and agreed to the marriage.

All the formalities were quickly completed in a week's time and the girl was married to her Rajasthani husband. He took her to Pune and soon she learnt about the lies of his riches and family.

For sometime he would bring strangers home and force her to sleep with them. And finally, he sold her to a brothel at Buddhawarpet in Pune and disappeared. Left alone in a strange city, her life became miserable – only a body without soul, a sexual object of desire. She was arrested and imprisoned for trafficking from Buddhawarpet. That is when I met her.

By that time, I had joined TV9, which had provided me with the opportunity to carry out sting operations for the first time in Karnataka. Many corrupt officials were exposed. I was determined to expose this trafficking business too. A friend of mine, Mehboob Munavalli, from Hubli district gave me information about a marriage broker, his name was Raju Mestri. By the time we reached Hubli, I had found a man, Prakash, to play the part of a groom. He was a camera person by profession. The interesting thing was we both had hidden cameras with us.

After three days of extensive search we managed to meet Raju Mestri. He owned a tractor garage. But basically, he was involved in trafficking of women. He was in contact with a number of marriage brokers in the area and also had a list of poor girls.

By the time we met him, I had explained to Prakash his role in the operation. Raju Mestri first took us to Yellapur, his own village. Once we got there, he began to talk. By then, I had convinced him about us and our story. He agreed to show us the girls. 'To date, I have married 327 girls off. Now, it has become very difficult to make deals since the police has got a whiff of what is going on. We have to give them a commission, otherwise they will book case against us.' He suggested to take us to meet the girls directly. That's what we wanted too. We wanted to meet the mothers who were so helpless that they were even ready to sell their daughters. We wanted to understand the plight of these families.

From here Mestri took us to another agent called Ashok Ritti. This man was a local BJP leader and a relative of an ex-minister of the state. They took us to a house in Yellapur to meet a girl.

My friend Prakash and Munavalli interviewed the bride-to-be. She was badly shaken. I couldn't believe somebody was actually going to buy her. Raju Mestri called us out of the house and described the poverty of her family. We could buy the girl for Rs 1 lakh.

We received permission to talk to the girl's mother but she did not answer any of our questions. We wanted to talk to the girl but were not allowed till the deal was not finalised. We wanted to talk to her but Prakash reminded us our cameras were running low on battery and the natural light was not enough for our camera lens. So we asked Raju to show us some more girls the next day.

The next day, two brokers arrived at our lodging before dawn. We were taken to a village 16 kilometres from Yellapur and were introduced to a woman who was running a cooperative society, Streeshakti. She was supposedly in touch with 1,200 girls. I was taken aback to learn she was assisting the brokers in selling the girls to the 'grooms'. She called for a girl. We talked to her. Unfortunately, she (girl) was not aware of the fact that she was being sold. She had only been told that somebody had come to marry her. She was unmoved even when we revealed that we were paying the brokers for her.

I heard Raju Mestri speaking to the woman: 'I cannot demand more money since she is not fair, so let us close this deal at Rs 79,000.' He sounded like a shrewd businessman. Raju Mestri took us to another decent-looking house in Sirasi when we told him that we did not like the girl we had just met. This time we were shown a graduate who wanted to get married. We had a brief conversation with her.

'Are you aware that you are being sold?' we asked her.

'No, I am not,' she said.

'Are you ready for marriage?'

'Talk to my mother,' she said, and went away.

After we came out, Raju Mestri started to bargain. We told him we were meeting these girls as we wanted to send them to brothels. He was cool as cucumber as if he had always known that.

I had spent ten days in Hubli. The next day I returned to Bengaluru and got my camera recordings edited and the Hubli story was ready. The day after the telecast, my friend Munavalli rang me up from Hubli and told me in a victorious voice, 'Sir, police raid is going on in Hubli and Raju has been arrested.'

Prakash was happy too. But I knew police would arrest some people but they would soon be out on bail.

While I was receiving the Ramnath Goenka Award, the Hubli police had arrested one such team. In a genuine case, a Rajasthani groom had gone to find a bride, but he was given a girl from a brothel for Rs 2 lakh. Within fifteen days of the marriage she left her husband and returned to Hubli. When the husband insisted she come back to him, she lodged a case of dowry against him. This is an evil practice in our society. We have to fight heart and soul to eradicate it.

Mridu Bhandari

Mridu Bhandari, 26, is Senior Associate Producer with ET NOW. She was with CNN-IBN when she won this award.

Mridu Bhandari looks at two terrible social injustices in north India: the bangle industry in Ferozabad, the brass industry in Moradabad and carpet weaving in Mirzapur, employ children; while two decades after manual scavenging was banned, it is rampant in parts of Madhya Pradesh.

SHAME
Personal Account

I still clearly remember the night before Day 1 of our week-long shoot at Gohad, Madhya Pradesh. I was apprehensive and slightly nervous like I usually am before any shoot; preparing my checklist of shots that cannot be missed, making a list of the people who need to be interviewed – the scavenger women, local government officials, human rights commission, activists, et al.

The day began early at 3.00 a.m. We were staying at a plush hotel in Gwalior, one hour away from Gohad and in order to catch the women going to work at 5.00 a.m., we had to be up and about really early. Throughout that one-hour drive, I was upbeat about going to the village – it always excites me to visit rural India, talk to villagers, listen to their numerous stories and I am always astounded by their awareness and intelligence despite their lack of education. But when we started shooting and following the women while they picked up other people's excreta, believe me, there was none of that excitement that I feel on other rural shoots. It was shocking. It was repulsive. It made me want to throw up.

On the second day of the shoot, we were met by a hostile group of women. All the women we had arranged to interview the previous day, refused to come on camera today. I was bewildered. They had seemed so warm and forthcoming the day before so why were they suddenly so hostile? Talking to other villagers, we realised the men of the village had convinced them that coming on camera would make them lose their jobs. They were scared that if the documentary was aired, they would lose their jobs. It is not easy being a Valmiki and an untouchable – all jobs except

Human scavengers are on the lowest rung of the social hierarchy, who for centuries have had the dehumanising task of collecting human excreta.

scavenging are meant for people from higher castes. In addition, they have no access to village facilities like the water well, the village tea shop, the village barber etc. It took us over two hours of counselling, cajoling and ultimately convincing them that the end of manual scavenging would mean a new beginning for them. I remember telling them that unless the urban, educated people *saw* with their own eyes the dehumanising practice of manual scavenging, no one would understand their plight, no one would be able to even imagine the trauma they go through. Then there were other villagers who felt we were commercial filmmakers come to exploit them, to make money by shooting with them. It took us a while to convince them that we were there with the aim of trying to give them a better life by showing the world what they are condemned to do for a living. In hindsight, I don't know if my report made a difference or contributed at all towards their development considering the local government outrightly refused to accept the presence of even a single manual scavenger in Gohad! But we journalists are always living in the hope that somewhere, sometime, somehow our efforts are making a positive difference.

In the next few days I met many scavenger women. Most of them had taken up the practice after they got married. I felt it's a strange legacy for a mother-in-law to pass on to her daughter-in-law. It was even stranger that they never let their daughters do this job but expected their daughters-in-law to do it with ease. Women who had been scavenging for years, were now resigned to their fate, they no longer showed any trace that they find the practice repulsive. Bhuri, a manual scavenger said very matter-of-factly, 'In the beginning I used to cry, I would vomit, I hated the foul smell but now it's not a problem, I'm used to it.' Over the years they have lost track of their dignity, self-respect and the discomfort of doing this task – all they can see is that there is no other form of employment and they have children to feed and a household to run. Being at the bottom of the caste ladder is not easy. Not only are manual scavengers treated as untouchables, they are also paid very meagre wages for this revolting job – a mere Rs 10-20 per month and 'rotis' that they have to beg everyday from the they clean. Most men in the village just sit around drinking and gambling all day long. They are casual labourers, often unemployed for most part of the month and don't mind their wives running the household. In Navrol village in Madhya Pradesh, manual scavengers are paid in kind – they are given foodgrains in exchange for their services but when we visited the village, we learnt the crop had been failing for the last two years and they weren't even paid for picking up excreta and cleaning toilets for two whole years. One scavenger woman had tried giving up this practice and even got a job as an Anganwadi helper but the villagers refused to send their children to her simply because she was a Valmiki by caste. In fact, a village priest – a Brahmin by caste – openly said on camera that to mix up with the Valmiki community is an unthinkable sin.

My meeting with Bismillah, a resident of Gohad, enraged me. She strongly believes in god, belongs to the minority community and is discriminated against by the residents of her locality, because of her faith. I'd expect someone like her to be more understanding towards the plight of manual scavengers and not discriminate on the basis of caste since she herself had been through similar circumstances. But she shamelessly said on camera that 'if manual scavengers give up this practice, who would clean the toilets of the upper-class community?' I was speechless. Perhaps it isn't Bismillah's fault. Lack of education, lack of a supportive society and age-old beliefs in the caste system have conditioned her mind and those of millions around her. At times like these, I feel it is difficult to remain an objective journalist and to not turn activist!

It is a fine line that at times I feel should be crossed so as to bring about a change in mindsets.

That whole week I felt like I was living in two parallel worlds – spending all day with women who are victims of the worst kind of caste oppression and returning to a plush hotel every night – one almost felt guilty of living in the comfort and luxury after seeing other people being denied even basic human rights. The shoot conditions were tough – to begin at 4 a.m. every day with the sight and smell of human excreta, following scavenger women and filming them picking up the filth wasn't exactly a pleasant experience, but was an eye opener. My cameraperson shot with utmost patience, never once complaining of the nauseating smell, the unearthly working hours or the long, tiring spells of travelling across villages in Madhya Pradesh – just watching these women at work made us feel that theirs is a story that must be told and told to bring about a change. The checklist of shots was long forgotten because here was a story that was just simply told from the heart and that I think came across in the way it was shot.

Manual scavenging is deeply rooted in caste but the infrastructure in Gohad is crumbling as well. In 2003, the Madhya Pradesh government promised to connect all dry toilets to a drainage system. But in Gohad, there is no sign of any drainage, dry toilets are still in use and the Mehtar or Valmiki community is expected to clean them. What shocked me the most was that manual scavenging does not only exist in the back of beyond. We found the practice prevalent even in the national capital! In Nand Nagri in Delhi, many women have been scavenging for over two decades. Sudha has still not forgotten the stench of her first encounter with manual scavenging twenty-five years ago. Over the years, the foul smell has crept into her system and she has developed respiratory problems. Most scavengers end up with asthma, tuberculosis or jaundice, many succumb to them and many others take to alcohol to get over the stench.

The government's rehabilitation programme for manual scavengers does not look at holistic development for them. The one-time cash grant only makes them spend the money and go back to scavenging. There is no emphasis on generation of any alternate employment by giving them vocational training or enhancing any kind of skills. Many states have not even adopted the 1993 Act for prohibition of manual scavenging and many deny the existence of manual scavengers yet receive funds for their rehabilitation. There is clearly a lack of political will to end the practice.

But my shoot in Gohad did not entirely comprise depressing stories. There were some stories of hope as well. Ramvati – a short, petite woman tried the tall task of giving up manual scavenging. She gave up the practice and became a sweeper at the local police station. Initially, she was shunned by the villagers and still treated as an untouchable even though she had given up scavenging. But she never stopped trying. She found sweeping the local police station much more respectable than cleaning other people's toilets. I still remember her saying, '*aath ghante ka kaam hai par shaan ka kaam hai*' (It's an eight-hour job but at least it is respectable). Slowly, over the years, villagers accepted her into the community, allowed her access to the village well – a strict no-no for the Valmikis – and even treated her with respect. A similar story is that of Battobai from Malanpur, a woman full of courage and life. The local NGO inspired her to give up manual scavenging a few years ago and today she is the inspiration for many other scavenger women – she sings motivational songs in the local language that send out a message to give up manual scavenging. At the end of her interview, Battobai took me by the arm and made me dance as well – her courage, her hope and the spirit with which she sang and danced are still fresh in my mind and even today, she continues to inspire other women to give up scavenging and live a respectable life.

Child, Interrupted!

'Child, Interrupted' was one of my first reporting assignments – a weeklong series of reports on child labour – an issue very close to my heart and something I feel very strongly about. So when my editor said we were doing this series for Children's Day, I was more than happy to be made the reporter and producer in-charge. At the time, I had very elementary knowledge of the subject and my work began with extensive research, meeting people who have for long fought for child rights and understanding the laws governing child labour. We decided to approach the issue industry-wise. Every day we would focus on one industry that has child labour and air a report on it. Out of these reports, three in northern India were given to me while three others were filed by reporters from the south.

Knot for Children, Mirzapur, Uttar Pradesh

My first stop was Mirzapur, a small town in Uttar Pradesh famous for its carpets – it exports carpets worth several thousand crore rupees every year and is world famous for its quality of weaves. But few people know of the little hands that weave these carpets. Carpet weaving is a home-based industry here and more often than not, the children of the family are also pulled into weaving – first to 'help' parents and soon they are working for the same number of hours or even more.

Mirzapur is a predominantly Muslim locality where residents have large families and their thought process is simple: the more the hands at work, the higher the family income. With this mindset, parents believe in having more number of children so they can be put to work from their early years and increase the family income. Even at the tender age of six to seven years, children are robbed of their childhood and are made to sit at looms in dingy, dark rooms and forced to weave carpets from dawn to dusk because their nimble fingers work with more ease as compared to adult fingers. Four to five children sit huddled together on wooden planks weaving carpets for about 10 hours every day for little or sometimes no wages at all. Children here suffer from severe backaches, weak eyesight and asthma because of sitting at looms for long hours without proper light or air.

Employers break the minimum wage law with impunity. They treat the family as a single labourer, no matter how many members of the family are employed in weaving the carpet. A carpet that sells for over Rs 1 lakh in Europe takes a family of three nearly four months to weave. They get Rs 8,000 for the job, which is just Rs 22 per day while the law sets a limit of Rs 120 per day.

It is not that people are unaware – in many areas in Mirzapur, I met parents who were fully aware that child labour is a punishable offence, and in these areas we were forced to use hidden cameras because they'd shoo away children from the looms on seeing a video camera. Despite knowing that robbing children of their innocence and forcing them to work is a crime, they rarely feel remorse even when their own children are working. For them, their sustenance is all that matters, the price of childhood notwithstanding.

Little Shine, Moradabad, Uttar Pradesh

Twelve-year-old Rahil had eyes that shone when he spoke. The smoke at the furnace was hurting his eyes and he coughed off and on but was excited about talking to a television crew. He excitedly explained how he works in the casting process of making brass products. In all his innocence, he had no idea that working at a brass furnace was taking away his childhood from him, depriving him of all the things a child must get during his growing up years. In addition, he was being subjected to grave danger while working with molten brass. Thousands of children like Rahil work in the brassware industry of Moradabad in Uttar Pradesh and are paid anything between Rs 7-15 per day.

When I first met nine-year-old Bilal, I wished I could adopt him! He was one of the most adorable kids I had ever met. A little boy with chubby cheeks, a squeaky voice and a smile that could capture any heart, Bilal had been forced to rotate the wheel at the brass furnace for hours everyday. This action maintains the furnace temperature but exposes the child to fumes and smoke. Bilal has developed a skin ailment all over his body as a result of working with metal. The local NGO that was fighting for child rights in Moradabad came to his rescue and decided to educate him. When I interviewed Bilal, he said in his sweet voice, 'I want to study, grow up and become a doctor.'

Hopefully, that dream will come true someday with the NGO stepping in to ensure he does not work again and regularly attends school.

Moradabad is very backward in terms of literacy rate, infrastructure and socio-economic development. There is no emphasis on education and abject poverty has forced parents to think of children as only a means to add to the household income. Many parents said they do feel bad about sending their children to work but are helpless and have no option because their own income is so low and they have a large family to feed. Brass furnace owners don't mind taking advantage of the situation. As Shamshad Hussain said, 'When I can get a young boy for Rs 30-40 per day, why will I hire an adult for Rs 100 a day?' Manufacturers know they have outwitted the law. They do not have stringent checks while outsourcing work to families to ensure that children do not work from homes.

The Rs 3000 crore brassware industry was declared hazardous for children over two decades ago but it continues to exploit children even today. The smoke at the casting unit continues to sting Rahil's eyes but thankfully, it hasn't diminished the twinkle in them, not just yet!

Brittle Childhood, Firozabad, Uttar Pradesh

I have always been a bangle lover, ever since I was a little girl. I could never cross a bangle shop without buying a dozen bangles for myself. So when I walked into India's glass town – this little place called Firozabad, located about 50 kilometres from Agra, the place was nothing short of paradise for me – all around, I could see *thelas* (carts) being pushed around, full of different coloured glass bangles. I was instantly tempted to buy dozens of these bangles. But I was on professional duty and we had a shoot to do. Little did I know then, of the stark reality behind these pretty glass bangles. Once in the interiors of Firozabad, we walked through many winding lanes to reach twelve-year-old Seema's house. She was sitting at a kerosene flame, joining pieces of glass to make them into round bangles. At first sight, one might think, what is so difficult about doing this? But soon the smoke from the flame starts to bother you and the smell of kerosene gets to you. Out of curiosity, I decided to sit at the flame and try joining bangles myself. I burnt my hand thrice and yet could not do the task properly. Little Seema then took over and did a professional job of it. She has been doing this since she was all of six years old. Children like her sit at the gas flames for 8-10 hours everyday – even though most of them go to school as well. Their parents wake them up at 4.00 a.m., only to put them to work at the kerosene flame. Soon after they return from school, they are back to work, joining more bangles. Seema is paid a meagre wage of Rs 2-2.50 for joining 256 bangles! Local activists say more than 40,000 children in the area work in the glass bangle industry and most suffer from tuberculosis, asthma and other respiratory diseases because of inhaling kerosene smoke for long hours everyday. Children are also employed for straightening and decorating bangles and paid as little as Rs 6 for decoration of every 100 bangles. Little girls sit for hours, trying to decorate bangles by sticking glitter on them with great precision. As a result many of them suffer from weak eyesight and severe backache. The years these children should spend playing, studying and learning are spent trying to earn for their families and in return, they often fall sick for life.

They say there is rarely a glass bangle in Firozabad that hasn't gone through the hands of a child while being manufactured. Ever since, whenever I hold a glass bangle and see its joint, I wonder which little kid spent his/her childhood on it and the temptation to buy it is far lesser.

With 23 million child workers, India is the sixth most unsafe country in the world for children. In all of the industries that I visited – be it carpet weaving, glass bangles or brassware – children are employed by shifting these industries to homes. All of these industries are classified as hazardous and employing children under the age of fourteen years in factories is a punishable offence but when the same children 'help' their parents at home, they are not even recognised as child labour. Another common problem is the exploitative wage system. Till the time skilled workers are not recognised and given their worth, they will continue to earn by sending their children to work. But most of all, it is the lack of political will to end child labour, to treat it as a social problem and offer long-term solutions. How else can one explain thousands of working children despite a two-decade old ban on child labour?

Nagendar Sharma

Nagendar Sharma, 37, is Associate Editor with the *Hindustan Times*.

Neelesh Misra

Journalist, writer, as well as scriptwriter and lyricist, Neelesh Misra, 37, is Deputy Executive Editor with the *Hindustan Times*.

[One-fourth of the country is at war from within. Rs 58,000 crore had been allocated to insurgency affected areas and nearly half of it has not been used. Is insurgency a convenient excuse for misgovernance?]

CITIZENS VS MILITANTS: A BATTLE GONE WRONG

Award-winning Story

More than 50,000 people from 650 villages left their homes and now live in makeshift roadside shelters, guarded by police and paramilitary forces.

On the Andhra Pradesh border with Chhattisgarh, these are the haggard soldiers of a war gone wrong. As insurgencies spread, from Kashmir to Jharkhand to Manipur and Chhattisgarh, governments armed the people to fight militants and protect themselves. The results have been mostly disastrous. Villagers have become vulnerable to gruesome revenge attacks by militants in the absence of training and guidance from the security forces.

In Chhattisgarh, the worst affected by Naxalites, a controversial two-year-old movement called Salwa Judum (People's Movement) has set off a furious cycle of conflict, with spiralling casualties. It was aimed at preparing the mainly tribal villagers to fight Naxalites by vacating their villages and living instead in tents close to police posts.

But hundreds have died in their clashes with Naxalites, tens of thousands are staying away from their homes – and still losing lives to rebels or bullets of security forces.

'We have been facing Naxalite attacks regularly. They burnt the newly constructed houses in camps and have threatened to kill us,' said Soyam Muka, president of the Konta Project, the biggest relief camp.

In the relief camps, residents sit idle with no source of income, surviving on government rations.

'I want to return to my village and see my land, but security

Salwa Judum, the people's movement, aimed at preparing mainly tribal villagers to fight Naxalites, has set off a furious cycle of conflict and spiralling casualties.

forces tell me I will be killed by the Naxalites the moment I return to my village,' said Mohammad Illyas, a middle-aged farmer in Dornapal relief camp in Dantewada district.

'It is better to die from a bullet rather than die in such a camp where I have nothing.'

In Jharkhand, groups of armed citizens called Nagrik Suraksha Samiti were formed in 2003. Thirteen Naxalites were killed that year by village groups led by women in Lango village in Orissa.

'Since then, Maoists have not been spending too much time in villages. They do their business and leave,' said Shailendra Singh Burnwal, deputy superintendent of police involved in anti-rebel operations. 'It was the biggest experiment by villagers, it was their local initiative. We gave them arms licenses.'

These villages soon became sites for bloodbaths. Many Naxalites were gored with arrows, and their bodies slashed with axes. The militants retaliated. In one incident that created waves across Jharkhand, tribal headman Jeevan Masih Bhuiyan was brutally beaten in public, his body hacked with an axe, and then burnt.

In Manipur, Village Defence Committees (VDCs) seemed to have found a solution in the early 1990s. But eventually they provoked more conflict as armed tribal militias clashed with each other to settle scores.

The only place where the system has worked with relative success is Jammu and Kashmir, where villagers in remote Hindu-majority areas in Jammu were armed. But the concept failed in the hub of insurgency, the Kashmir Valley.

'The VDC system is working very well. We have not witnessed any terrorist activity in those areas,' said Kuldip Khoda, additional director-general of police. 'In the Valley, it did not take off.'

The Salwa Judum movement, described as a spontaneous 'people's movement', is fully supported by the Raman Singh government in Chhattisgarh and is being run under the guidance of Mahendra Karma, a powerful tribal leader of the Opposition Congress. Some 57,000 villagers now live in twenty-three relief camps. In a series of clashes, 750 people died last year.

'Higher casualties in Chhattisgarh are due to the Naxalite-Salwa Judum confrontation and proactive counter-operations by security forces against Naxalites. Overall, Naxal violence in the country has shown a decline in 2006,' the Ministry of Home Affairs said.

Karma dismisses the criticism. 'Anywhere in the world where people have faced political terror, displacement has taken place. In Chhattisgarh, it is positive displacement that has strengthened the resolve of the people to fight Naxalites. We are fighting for victory and small things do not bother us,' he said.

Many disagree. The move to recruit villagers as special police officers (SPOs) is especially running into tough opposition and critics say that could pitch tribals against their own community.

Personal Account
Nagendar Sharma

It is easier for journalists to write their stories rather than writing about themselves and how they do their stories. Here I am making an attempt.

It was sometime in May 2007, within weeks of my joining the *Hindustan Times* (HT), that I was sitting with Neelesh, in his room, and talking about a possible series we could do together.

Frankly, it was his idea, which we worked upon for a couple of weeks to put out the brief for our editors, it was the new buzzword in HT: give a brief of what you want to do. I was new to all this, having spent six years in the world of broadcasting, I was struggling to get back to the basics of print media once again. Believe me, jumping straight into a big newspaper, when you are switching medium, is not a very good idea.

I joined HT in April 2007, after having worked for the BBC World Service, Hindi, for six years. My bosses at the BBC, both in London and Delhi, told me broadcasting came naturally to me, though I had started my journalism career with the PTI in 1998.

My bosses at BBC were perplexed when I decided to quit the organisation, they asked me for the reason, which I really did not have. I politely told them I wanted to do something else. My immediate boss, Sanjeev Srivastava, tried to persuade me, but was nice enough to give me a dream recommendation letter, so did Mark Tully, without even knowing me well!

Sanjeev's predecessor, Seema Chishti, who had left the BBC a year earlier, felt the world outside was worth giving it a try. I still feel, my London bosses Achala Sharma and Neil Curry, were not happy with the decision, though I am not sure whether they were entirely happy with my work. They indirectly gave me the option of returning to London, but I had made up my mind.

The only person who was happy was Sam Miller, the former South Asia managing editor of the BBC World Service (better known in India for his book on Delhi). I still remember Sam telling me, 'Jump into real journalism, you will enjoy it.'

This encouraged me, since Sam was in the interview board in the year 2000, which had selected me for the BBC job.

Then HT editor-in-chief, Chaitanya Kalbag, who hired me, after several rounds of meetings, told me he expected investigative stories to be done in the paper. The initial days were frustrating, it took HT fifteen days to decide my date of joining. My first story for HT appeared on the front page, it was about Akash Missile system being slammed by experts. Next day there were many in-house experts/pundits in the internal morning meeting, who proudly trashed the story of their new colleague. This was April-end, I was unable to produce much for the next month or so in the intimidating atmosphere.

Coming back to the series, after much persuasion and a couple of rewritten briefs, Neelesh and I were given the go-ahead for the series 'on a shoe-string budget'.

We decided to focus on insurgency as an excuse for non-governance. The idea was to get a big picture of what was happening in the remote corners of the country, specially disturbed areas, for one reason or the other.

My focus was on Naxalism, however, it was Neelesh who insisted on also including the Northeast and Kashmir to make our work more broad-based. Both of us thought it would be better to first travel, get an initial picture of what was happening and then compare our notes to bring out the final story. Our research from government document brought out an amazing fact – one in six Indians is living under insurgency, their lives shaped by militancy, violence and fear.

Armed with this finding, we set out to find the reasons. Neelesh decided to travel to Jammu and Kashmir; the Maoist-infested Jharkhand belt; and Manipur. I decided to travel to the Maoist-infested Andhra-Chattisgarh belt and Nagaland.

We decided to finish the touring by the third week of June,

since we were keen to bring out the series of stories from the beginning of July. My keenness was based on the reason that I had managed only three stories in my first two months in HT.

I decided to first go to Hyderabad, meet some prominent Maoist ideologues, pick up some contacts and then travel by road from Andhra to Chattisgarh.

My last visit to Hyderabad was to cover the All India Congress Committee session in January 2006. It was bustling with activity then, with the country's who's who present there, and journalists were treated like VIPs.

Here I was in June 2007 again, alone and lost this time. My dear friend and former BBC colleague, Omar Farooq was ever helpful, but not enthused by the topic I had chosen for the series. With slight hesitation he told me, 'Don't you think you are slightly late on the series? Andhra government has forced the Naxalites to leave the state. They are now either in jungles of Chattisgarh or Jharkhand.'

I spent the day meeting the famous balladeer Gaddar, one of the few Naxal ideologues, who sings and lives in public domain. I tried meeting top state officials to get a sense of what they felt about the problem in the state. Probably Omar was right, because a majority of them were dismissive of the whole thing.

Next day, I started my road journey towards Chattisgarh, taking the Khammam route. My taxi driver was my guide, who talked a lot, but knew little.

A local photographer in Khammam was kind enough to waste his time on me. He showed me some places damaged in Naxal attacks and provided me the photographs I asked for.

I decided to proceed to the temple town Bhadrachalam to spend the night and cover as much distance as possible to be close to the Chattisgarh-Orissa-Andhra border.

After spending a relaxed night, I started early the next day since I wanted to reach Chintoor, the last point of Andhra before crossing over to Chattisgarh.

Within three hours I was there and started looking for a local journalist, Vijay. My meeting with him turned out to be one of the most interesting in my life.

He was sitting in his shop, in this small town, which did not have more than ten shops. After reaching his shop and exchanging pleasantries, I explained my motive of coming to this far-flung town. Vijay seemed disinterested, offered me tea and said all journalists come from Delhi in search of special and not real stories. Sensing that he meant business, I offered him lunch, which he readily agreed to and suggested we go to a roadside dhaba, which were there in plenty.

Once settled, he ordered beer and wanted some to be reserved for his dinner too. After a couple of glasses, he opened up and said he could arrange a meeting with some Naxal leaders. This was what I wanted, but my joy was short-lived since he said it would take a few days for him to arrange it and if I wanted I could return from Raipur.

I got a sense there that people were living in fear, but had no hope from the government. Vijay introduced me to many villagers and agreed to accompany me to a few Salwa Judum camps on Chattisgarh border. Crossing over into the tribal areas of Chattisgarh, he told me that dense forests on both sides of the road were Naxal hideouts. On the way, the road was blocked by some tribal women who wanted five rupees for some local festival.

The situation in these camps was alarming, poor villagers who fled their homes and lands, were living in miserable conditions. The villagers in these camps were being guarded by Naga and Mizo policemen. Local boys were armed with guns, I was told they were the Special Police Officers under the much publicised and controversial Salwa Judum programme of the Chattisgarh government. It was a different world I was in, poor tribal women, nude till their waists were rushing back to their camps with loads of wood and grass on their heads.

It was getting dark and Vijay suggested we return to Chintoor and start in the morning for Dantewada (Chattisgarh). However, I paid him his taxi fare to return and decided to proceed ahead.

The road was lonely, but my taxi driver said it was due to rain that there was less traffic. Two local journalists whom I had contacted from Delhi rang me and insisted on speaking to the driver. After he finished the conversation, the driver told me they were just guiding him. When we finally reached Dantewada, both Hemant Kashyap and Pawan Dubey (local journalists) told me the road is full of landmines and it was not a good idea to travel in dark. I did not understand the intensity of what they were saying, and jokingly told them let us buy our drink before the shops were shut. What I saw the next day was shocking. No government official stayed in the border district after 2 p.m., though the district collector, who himself left at 3 p.m. did not concede the point. Petrol was being sold illegally in plastic bottles. There was no electricity for almost a fortnight. According to the local residents, the Naxalites had blown up transformers in the entire Bastar belt, and it would take a week more to restore normalcy.

Infrastructure situation was not bad – roads were fine, there were schools and a college, whose roof had been blown up as part of the Naxals awareness campaign and surprisingly there were functional internet connections in the collector's office.

Senior Congress leader and one of the main protagonists of Salwa Judum, spoke highly of his initiative at a heavily guarded government rest house. 'This is one of the rare programmes in which there are no differences between the ruling and the opposition parties,' Karma said. After meeting many like Karma, I returned to my hotel, which had a generator. It was in remote Dantewada that I came to know that Pratibha Patil was likely to become the country's next president. Honestly, I did not know much about her expect that she was a governor of some state.

The mobile connection was playing tricks, but Neelesh managed to get through from Saranda hills of Jharkhand. He asked me how was it going? Not wanting to disappoint him, I replied, 'Very good'. The conversation was brief, but both of us sounded energetic.

I got a feeling that in the entire Bastar region, common people were not really interested in the government programmes. Yes, tribal villagers, whose lives were affected by the activities of Naxals and government operations, did not really know what was good for them. Before reaching Raipur, I went to Bijapur, and the situation there was even more serious than Dantewada.

The capital Raipur did not have much to offer, expect the government jargons and hearsay about Naxal activities.

I returned to Delhi after a week and tried to jot down my notes. Neelesh insisted that we complete the travelling part first, and a week later, I set off for Nagaland. The small plane from Kolkata to Dimapur had majority of Nagaland locals. I heard a young girl say, 'There are many Indians on the flight today.'

The moment I stepped out from the Dimapur airport, guntotting paramilitary forces personnel gave an indication of the prevailing situation. A Hindi speaking auto driver from Bihar said he knew my hotel and would take me there.

I had relatively better contacts in Dimapur and journalists Pradeep Parikh and Dilip Sinha were my guides. Though, they blunt my enthusiasm by saying that hopes of meeting insurgent group NSCN-IM group leaders were very grim.

They forced me to stay indoors as soon as it turned dark, but were nice enough to provide company for a couple of drinks before hurrying home.

Next morning, the journey from Dimapur to Kohima was a good drive. There was some commotion on the outskirts of Dimapur. A Hindi speaking fruit seller 'had been taught a lesson' for charging more for the fruits he was selling. Meetings with the chief minister and top state officials were formal – trashing the insurgents and saying their government was doing a great job.

After spending a couple of days in the far-flung state, I returned to Delhi, where Neelesh was eagerly waiting. Both of us got down to writing, but Neelesh had a tougher role as he anchored the series. I had the easier job of sending my bits to him.

The first part of the series was published on the front page – couple of newspapers, specially *Times of India,* helped by following up the story with an editorial the next day. That helped us push the first five-six parts without difficulty, it was at that point that the editors were getting tired – they did not like 600-700 word stories 'eating up a lot of space'.

We persisted, managed to get a nine-part series, but that was all. I had forgotten the series soon after it was over, but it was Neelesh who decided to send the entry for the prestigious Ramnath Goenka Award. I just signed the form and filled the mandatory columns.

I have, however, told him that I am his lucky mascot and in case he wants the next award, he must keep some role for me in his series plans.

Nidhi Razdan

Nidhi Razdan, 33, is Senior Anchor and Senior Special Correspondent with the NDTV 24x7.

[Like any other state, the youth of Kashmir want to move on. They want jobs. They want development. They have had enough of separatism and the ensuing violence.]

KASHMIR
Personal Account

Kashmir is special, its different, and its complex. It's my home. When I began my career ten years ago, this was a story I desperately wanted to cover. For my parents, the very first assignment on the eve of Independence Day 2000, was nerve wracking. That is because the last time we were all there was as a family in 1989. When the killings had just started, when a bomb went off right before our eyes outside a mithai shop in the heart of Srinagar, when we were told for the first time that we couldn't enter the Hazratbal shrine because we are pandits. Circa August 2000. My mother nervously told me not to wear a bindi, my father told me to pretend I was Punjabi! Even in those days, with far fewer 24x7 channels, let's just say I wasn't exactly inconspicuous when I arrived in Srinagar! I couldn't believe this was the same place I had last seen all those years ago. The security personnel, the curfews, the tension.

Ten years later, the Kashmir story has changed so dramatically. The documentary was a journey for me as well, to try and understand what those born during militancy think and feel, to try and understand the hostility towards the Indian state without being trapped by the boundaries of a 1 minute 30 second news item. In that summer of 2007, young men were demonstrating on the streets of Srinagar for jobs, not for azaadi. A well-known bank had begun trading on the stock market. A call centre had just come up. And did I mention the mall down the road from the legendary Ahdoos? Yes, Kashmir had changed. And yet so much had not. A large number of people still resented India; the sense of alienation was and is very deep. But there was also a universal feeling – that there is no more room for violence. And that it was time to get on with life as they continued to harbour the ideals of freedom. But for me, having been brought up on the idea of Kashmiriyat, I felt horribly sad as we filmed a section on whether young muslims, born after the insurgency, knew anything about pandits. So many do not even know Hindus are Kashmiri too. And when one college student told me she didn't really consider pandits 'Kashmiris', it took all my self-restraint not to scream!

I met so many amazing people while Ajmal Jami, our ace cameraman, and I filmed. The young woman radio jockey, the eighteen-year-old boy who had come to invest in the stock market, the thirty-something businessman who gave up a career abroad to come back home, the nearly ninety-year-old ex-forest officer who had watched J&K transform over the last sixty years, the young men in the villages who don't care for politics, only for jobs, the college boys who surprised me when they said President Kalam was their icon, and the young woman who said she wanted to join the IAS and was a proud Indian!

Another amazing story I have covered in the Valley in the last ten years was the Srinagar-Muzaffarabad bus service. It was April 2005. I was standing there, at the Kaman Post on the Line of Control, talking constantly on live TV as we waited for the bus.

Kashmir is different, it's complex and it's changing. A large number of people still feel a sense of alienation but there's also a universal feeling that there is no more room for violence.

But when the passengers began to cross the bridge, I couldn't speak. I was live, on air, and I was speechless. There was nothing I could have said to describe that moment. So on air, I just said, 'I am keeping quiet now to let this sink in.' Lesson in TV journalism number one: sometimes silence really does speak louder. I was flooded with letters after that assignment.

I also had the chance to travel to 'Azad Kashmir' and to Gilgit in the Northern Areas. Standing on the LoC from the Pakistani side, I could see Indian troops with the naked eye and we waved back and forth. It was surreal that here we were, just a few feet from each other, and yet so far.

24-hour television has some amazing moments too! I have covered many many stories for NDTV in the last ten years – from earthquakes to political thrillers – and many turned out to be marathon 24x7 events. Of course, the dynamics have changed as more news channels came on the scene. Most of those changes are not to my liking.

The hijacking of IC 814 was my first big story; my first chance to see 24-hour news at it's best, and worst. Even today, we debate how television coverage at the time affected the decision to release the terrorists. I have always believed it was unfair for the then government to point a finger at the messenger. No, I didn't cover '26/11' and so much has already been debated on that. But I do want to say to those who criticise TV news – television is a medium that can tell you a story like no other. Stories can be meaningful, in-depth and analytical. I know there are enough sensational channels out there causing you to raise your eyebrows! And much of your criticism is valid too.

I still have lots to learn. But this is my appeal to my fraternity: please don't let TV news become a soundbite, 'breaking news' circus. We do have stories to tell, real stories. Maybe I am too idealistic. But that's how I would rather be.

P Sainath

Winner of the Ramon Magsaysay award for journalism, literature, and creative communication arts, P Sainath, 52, is Rural Affairs Editor, *The Hindu*.

[Farmers are committing suicide in Vidarbha, Maharashtra, to the tune of seven a day. The world needs to sit up and take notice.]

THREE WEDDINGS AND A FUNERAL

Award-winning Story

In one third of Gosavi Pawar's house there was mourning. In another third, celebration. In the last part of his home there was preparation for both mourning and celebration. This Banjara household in Yavatmal had to conduct a funeral and three weddings in 24 hours.

Pawar was the eldest brother and head of the extended family. The 'bada-pitaji' or big father. 'In the Banjara samaj,' says Mohan Jadhav, 'the eldest brother accepts a major role in the marriages of his kin. And he had to perform two that week.' Jadhav is secretary of the Vidharbha Jan Andolan Samiti (VJAS) and helped steer the family through its crisis. 'Gosavi was deep in debt. As every farmer here is. Yet, he tried to get the weddings done.'

He was also one of the ten indebted farmers who killed themselves on 9 May. And among the 520 who have taken their lives since June last year in the region's ongoing agrarian crisis. The distress driving the deaths reflects in everything from cancelled weddings to funerals.

Pawar was deep in debt and had little money for the new farming season. He had even resorted to a 'khande palat' to raise the crop loan he required. That is, 'switching the burden from one shoulder to another'. He needed Rs 65,000 to work his seven acres. But owed the bank Rs 50,000, which he had to clear first. 'So,' says Kishore Tiwari of the VJAS, 'he took the latter amount from a moneylender at a charge of Rs 2500 – for just one day. He cleared his bank debt with that, got the crop loan and repaid the lender. This means he was left with just Rs 12,500. And a new debt of Rs 65,000.' Khande palat is common in the debt-ridden villages here.

Gosavi Pawar went on 8 May from his village of Koljhari to the town of Mohada. The wedding of Savita, daughter of one brother, was set for 9 May. That of Pramod, son of another brother, was fixed for 10 May. But Pawar never returned. 'I first learnt of his death from an auto driver,' says his son Prakash. 'My father had gone to Mohada to buy the clothes, garments and other gifts for the weddings.' But no merchant there was willing to extend him credit on the purchases. Already in despair over his debts, Pawar took his own life.

He was brought to the post-mortem centre in Yavatmal town. The police wanted the body removed quickly – post-mortem centres in Vidharbha are busy places. But the grieving family needed to delay bringing him home. 'How could they bring a dead body to a house where a wedding was on?' asks deputy sarpanch, Tulsiram Chavan. So the body's return was slowed down until the baraat had left the house. Despite this, body and baraat met at a junction. Pawar's pallbearers moved away into a field, behind a cluster of trees to avoid contact. But the bride Savita wept, knowing it was her 'Kaka's' last journey she was seeing at a distance.

There was still another wedding to go the next day. 'I wanted to postpone mine when I learnt uncle was dead,' says the bridegroom, Pramod Pawar. 'But the village pointed out that the bride's family and others would be put to huge losses. More so because another couple's marriage was also tied to mine to save money.' Vidharbha's crisis has seen many weddings called off. Few can afford them. The village elders knew that delay could mean cancellation. So, heartbroken, they went ahead.

'We were so disturbed by my brother's suicide, we could not even attend to our guests,' says Phulsingh, father of Pramod. 'I wanted to call it off.' That's when the residents of this debt-burdened village came to their rescue in a moving show of solidarity. People, as poor as the family and worse, contributed small sums and other help to see it through. 'We held a meeting that night to plan, and everybody chipped in,' says Chavan. 'Some took charge of the cooking. Others looked after the guests. A few arranged the funeral, yet others the transport.' And a village celebrated its grief. For many across this region, funerals and weddings now depend on the aid of neighbours whose economic condition might be more dismal than their own.

Savita was married on the 9. Her uncle's funeral took place the same evening. Her cousin Pramod's wedding took place on the 10, along with that of the last couple. The collective effort of the Banjara clans saw the family come through the ordeal. At least, for now.

The 80-plus Banjara families in this 'no-liquor' village have a collective debt of over Rs 22 lakh. Koljhari's agriculture is a picture of all that has gone wrong. Soaring costs, fake inputs, crashing output prices, growing debt and a collapse of formal credit. As with many others, Pawar's tryst with Bt cotton also proved a disaster. His seven acres yielded just four quintals. A crippling loss. Meanwhile, most adults here – and quite a few who are not – have sought work under the National Rural Employment Guarantee Programme. But nothing has happened so far.

Debt-related suicides in Vidharbha show no sign of slowing down. 'Nor are they likely to,' says Wamanrao Rathore in Koljhari. 'See, people have readied their fields for the new season. But no one has bought the inputs as yet. Who can afford them? The banks won't give them loans. How do they cultivate?'

The 520 suicides listed by the Vidharbha Jan Andolan Samiti since last June is the highest number recorded here since 1998. The 306 since January means there's one every ten hours now. While farm suicides doubled almost every year between 2001-04, the leap since last November has been huge. That's when it became clear the government would not reverse the cut in cotton price it had announced. Last year, the state withdrew its 'advance bonus' of Rs 500 a quintal. This brought down what the farmer received for cotton to the MSP of Rs 1700 a quintal. A move that has fed into and spurred disaster.

In Vidharbha's register of suicides, Pawar is just another statistic. Number 499. For Prakash and widow Kamlabai, he was father and husband. And yet, his death was not a complete surprise. 'Yes, we feared he might do this,' says Prakash. 'Anyone in our (farmers') condition could do this. I could also do this.'

PK Prakash

PK Prakash, 41, is Senior Correspondent with *Madhyamam Daily*, Kerala.

[The agricultural sector was in deep crisis in Kerala leading the farmers to suicide. PK Prakash's research shows that most of Kerala is linked with the global market hence stability of crop prices is essential to the survival of farmers.]

GAMBLES OF THE MARKET: FUTILITY OF THE PACKAGES

Award-winning Story

Mammachan Jacob became emotional talking about the miseries that 'black gold' put him through. He could not control his tears, and as his sobs became uncontrollable, he could not continue with the conversation; other farmers standing beside him began the story from where he left off. The story of a farmer who was jailed, as his pepper farms were devastated by the gambles of the market.

Manjappara, a village in Vazhathoppu gramapanchayath of Idukki district, is populated by immigrant farmers. Mammachan Jacob, a small-scale farmer, owns 1.5 acres of land here. Mammachan planted 1,500 best-quality pepper saplings and constructed all necessary infrastructure on his farmland in 1999, when pepper had record prices in the market – Rs 250 per kg. In order to start the cultivation, Mammachan had taken a loan from the agriculture development bank. In the three years that Mammachan had to wait to begin getting a yield, his saplings were infested, and he had to spend more on pesticides and fertilizers. Since he had pledged his land to the bank, and since the bank was not willing to provide him with any more loans, Mammachan had to borrow more money from private financiers. But Mammachan was optimistic, because pepper was getting record prices. All his loans can be repaid if he gets one good yield.

The downturn in the market not just shattered Mammachan's dreams, but his life itself. By 2002, when his plants became ready for harvest, pepper prices came down to Rs 60 per kg. He lost all hopes that his loans can be repaid and maintenance of saplings came down. He had already repaid Rs 17,000 as interest for the Rs 40,000 that he had borrowed from the private financier. When the monthly repayments stopped coming through, the private financier approached Idukki Munsif Court, which provided Mammachan with an option to pay a lump sum of Rs 5,000 immediately and to repay the rest of the loan in installments. However, Mammachan was not in a position to procure a sum of Rs 5,000, and was put behind bars in April 2005 for having missed repayment of the loan. He spent 25 days in Viyyur central prison, and upon release, had a strong inclination to commit suicide. But he exercised self-control as he thought about the future of his two children, who were studying in standards X and XI.

By this time, owing to poor maintenance, his pepper plants stopped yielding completely. Now, Mammachan is planting rubber in between pepper plants, because currently rubber has a good price. Will the rubber market cheat him by the time his plants begin yielding? Mammachan is not sure, but he does not have any other alternative.

In most of the houses in this village, there are no men and women of working age; only old people and children who have dropped out of school. As the prices of agricultural products came down, their incomes stopped, and unemployment set in. The men folk migrated to the neighbouring districts to seek employment in the construction industry and women in home nursing.

At Nedumkandom, we met Karivelil Lalu Dominic, aka George, who returned to India after working abroad for nine years. He bought 15 acres of land at Chathurangappara for farming. Most of his land was cultivated with pepper, and in 1996, he intensified pepper farming by taking a loan from the Nedumkandom branch of Malanad Agriculture Development Bank. In 2001, the price of pepper started coming down steeply and he cleared some land to cultivate cardamom, which still fetched good price, and would start yielding from the second year onwards. He planted saplings in 8 acres of land and constructed a store at an expense of Rs 6 lakh. The price of cardamom at that time was Rs 900 per kg but by the time he started getting yield, it came down to Rs 200; now it has risen again to Rs 400.

Meanwhile, the cost of pesticides and fertilizers increased steeply. Cow dung, which used to cost Rs 2 per tin when George started his farm, went up to Rs 12; the cost of labour went up from Rs 60 to Rs 125; the cost of pesticide went up from Rs 280 to Rs 500 per litre. After spending huge amount on pesticides, fertilizers, and labour, the only thing left to harvest was loss.

The cost of Sulphur, a main component of bordeaux mixture which is used as a pesticide in cardamom plantations, was Rs 60 when George started his plantation, and it went up to Rs 170; lime which was Rs 40 per 10 kg, saw its cost go up to Rs 70. When the price of cardamom came down from Rs 900 to Rs 200 and then Rs 400, agriculture expenses increased twofold.

After having suffered insurmountable losses in agriculture, George had decided to return to Dubai to look for work again, when vanilla farming started making inroads in Kerala. The raw vanilla beans used to fetch above Rs 3,000 per kg in the market, and the cost of a sapling was Rs 100. In 2002, the Spices Board promised the farmers that the price of vanilla would never come down. Farmers celebrated the rise in price of vanilla by protecting it with fierce bloodhounds, electrified fences, and overnight security. Even the wood stumps that were used as supports for the creepers started fetching good prices. After having burnt their fingers in the gambles of pepper and cardamom markets, George decided to try his luck once again by planting 3,000 vanilla saplings, at a cost of Rs 190,000. But when it started yielding, the market cheated George once again by bringing down the price of vanilla from Rs 3,000 to Rs 200 per kg at one go; currently it fetches Rs 70 per kg and moreover there are only a few takers for vanilla! Currently, George is on the verge of suicide. His loan amount has increased many-fold with interests and cumulative interests, and the farmer is preparing to go back to Gulf to avoid suicide.

Once upon a time, the high-yielding terrains of Wayanad, Idukki, and Palakkad district were the farmers' dreamlands. However, the current scenario is that of the farmer who has lost his foothold in the gambles of the market created by the Agreement on Agriculture (AoA) of the World Trade Organisation (WTO).

Personal Account

There was a significant rise in farmer suicides in Kerala during 2005-07. Looking at the statistics I realised that the agricultural sector in Kerala was in deep crisis. The figures compelled me to study the problem in detail and look at the reasons behind it.

Gambles of the market, dealing with globalisation and how it impact, even the remotest corner of the countryside were some of the issues. The series of articles on the subject dealt with the unstable global market. The inconsistency of the market leads to misery, insecurity and wastage of resources.

Most of the crops of Kerala are for the global market. Hence the stability of crop price is essential for the existence of farmers. Any number of agricultural packages without assuring price stability will never help the farmers.

For this purpose I travelled through the major agricultural districts of Kerala, like Idukki, Alappuzha, Palakkad and Wayanad. I witnessed the pathetic situation in which farmers were trying to survive. I also met with the families of the farmers who have committed suicide. My travels lasted more than one month on the soil that smells of the death of farmers.

P Vaidyanathan Iyer

P Vaidyanathan Iyer, 37, is National Business Editor, *The Indian Express*. He won this award for his cover story for *Business World*.

[Even now, people may not want to address the economic slow-down. But it is imperative to look beyond the obvious.]

ECOMONY SLOW GOING

Award-winning Story

A Martian economist – if there is such a thing – who landed in India would have a hard time making sense of the schizophrenia that seems to have gripped us. This week, the Bombay Stock Exchange Sensitive Index (Sensex) flirted with a new record high of 18,000. If it had closed at that level, it would have been the fastest 2000-point rise in the recent history of any stock market. In the past few weeks, this has been the story dominating the headlines of newspapers here and overseas.

In the middle of the sea of stock market news, there have been economy data releases that tell a different story. For the past four months, the index of industrial production (IIP) has been declining steadily, falling from 13.6 per cent in April to 7.1 per cent in July. The IIP may continue the decline in August. 'But can it become a precipitous slide?' asks Subir Gokarn, chief economist for Asia Pacific at Standard & Poor's, adding that it may possibly be a slow landing, but not a slowdown.

At various industry association seminars and meetings, company chiefs have been complaining about high interest rates, and the cost of credit. Export firms have been pleading for the Reserve Bank of India (RBI) to stem the appreciation of the exchange rate as their margins were being eroded. Inflationary pressures seem to be showing up, driven by capital flows that are rising to dramatic levels. The signs have been emerging for some time now; but the barometer of optimism that is the stock market threatens to drown even the mildest suggestions of a deceleration in economic growth.

Are We Headed For A Slowdown?

After recording a stellar 25 per cent compounded annual growth rate over the past five years, sales of medium and heavy commercial vehicles – a leading indicator – fell for the first time by over 5 per cent during April-August of this year. 'One explanation for that could be that most trucking companies have finished replenishing their fleets,' says Gokarn.

The freight revenues of the Indian Railways – it carries almost a third of the country's total freight (the balance is carted by road) – grew by a modest 10 per cent during the same period, compared with a robust 15 per cent in the first five months last fiscal. Granted, a single number like the IIP does not a trend make. Many in government and outside it dismiss the sluggish industrial production figures of July as just a deviation; economists have offered similar explanations for the poor showing in several manufacturing sectors during April-July this year – metal products and parts, transport equipment, intermediate goods. Remember, industry contributes about a fifth to the country's gross domestic product (GDP) and a slippage here will take a while to correct.

There are signs that consumption is slowing in certain ways too. The IIP's consumer durables segment also showed a decline, though it has been contested by the companies who question the robustness of the IIP and its current weights. 'The decline in consumer goods growth is to be expected, given the slowdown in retail credit growth,' says Manika Premsingh, economist at Edelweiss Capital.

Whither Investment-led Growth?

Both, the Prime Minister's Economic Advisory Council and the Ministry of Finance stress that GDP growth over the next three years will be fuelled by investments. They point out that India is making a transition from a demand-led growth of the past three years to strong investment-led growth. Yes, India grew at a stupendous rate of 8.4 per cent during the past three years in the backdrop of low interest rates and moderate inflation that boosted consumer-led spending.

GDP growth at 9.3 per cent in the first quarter of 2007-08 fuelled optimism – despite a series of monetary tightening measures in the second half of last year – that India would finally catch up with China and post double-digit economic growth. But that may have been putting the cart before the horse. 'Our boom was consumption-led,' says Pronab Sen, chief statistician for the government of India. 'Investments followed, and are continuing. The slowdown in consumption began in late February-early March this year. There is a lag of 7-8 months before it reflects on investment.' But Sen says there will be reasons to worry only if the consumption numbers continue to fall beyond November.

But there are several supply-side constraints – long-term in nature – that require government intervention and policy initiatives. Infrastructure sectors, including power, require urgent attention, but cannot be addressed overnight. Other supply-side measures such as cuts in import duty where shortages are visible, or liberalized imports (like in the case of wheat) can help solve problems, but simultaneously raise other concerns with regard to food prices.

So how far will GDP growth decline? A consensus forecast seems to be emerging around 8.5 per cent, a rate that the RBI has suggested was likely early this year. Expectations of corporate profitability remain high, which will be the single largest driver of investment. And many companies have used external commercial borrowings (ECBs) to finance both acquisitions and planned greenfield projects. Capital goods show a slightly mixed trend, in part driven by imports aided by an appreciating rupee. To the extent capital goods drive industrial activity, there does not appear to be a cooling off. Imports have also managed to keep manufacturing inflation moderate, and prices down, even during a commodity cycle upswing.

Bulls and Bears

Key Takes on the State of the Economy

Bulls

Who: Finance Minister P Chidambaram
When: Reacting to the sluggish July IIP figures
What: No conclusion can be drawn from one month's figures. IIP figures for July are disappointing, but do not read too much at this stage. My outlook is positive.

Who: Asian Development Bank
When: In its Asian Development Outlook released in September
What: Indian economy will expand by 8.5 per cent in 2007 and

2008, up from an earlier forecast of 8 and 8.3 per cent, respectively, on robust investment, buoyant industrial expansion and moderate agricultural growth.

Who: Citigroup

When: In its India Economy Flash note released in September

What: We maintain our full year 9.3 per cent GDP estimate as the infrastructure slowdown is largely supply driven, agriculture could surprise on the upside and a relatively benign monetary policy environment that should stem further decline in consumption.

On The Fence

Who: Planning Commission Deputy Chairman Montek Singh Ahluwalia

When: In response to queries if India was heading for a slowdown

What: We have been predicting a slightly lower growth and the latest industrial output numbers are no reason to reassess the growth estimate. I would rather call it a moderation in growth rather than a slowdown.

Bears

Who: ICICI Bank MD & CEO KV Kamath

When: Reacting to July IIP figures

What: The slowdown in IIP is an amber signal. Policymakers will have to take a call on interest rates as a slowdown in growth rate will make it difficult to regain momentum.

Who: Moody's Economy.com Asia Pacific Director Ruth Stroppiana

When: Reacting to queries on her report, 'The Elephant's charge expected to slow.'

What: We expect India to switch to a slower growth path over the next few years. Real GDP is expected to moderate to 8.5 per cent in 2007 and 7.9 per cent in 2008.

Who: HSBC Global Research

When: In September issue of India Watch

What: We can't be confident that the economy is out of the woods… we are looking for a 7 per cent increase in 2008-09.

Importing More Than Capital

But a continuous appreciation of the rupee has made India's exports uncompetitive in the global market. This year alone, the rupee has appreciated 10 per cent against the US dollar to breach the Rs 40-mark. C Rangarajan, chairman of the PM's Economic Advisory Council, expects it to still grow 18 per cent this fiscal, which some see as an optimistic assessment. 'For every 1 per cent cut in our exports, we need a 10 per cent increase in consumption,' says Sen. This may not be possible unless the government intervenes by stepping up public expenditure to address the demand side. Commerce and Industry Minister Kamal Nath had estimated in his annual review of the Foreign Trade Policy this year that merchandise exports will touch $160 billion (Rs 6,40,000 crore) in 2007-08, 25 per cent more than the $126 billion (Rs 5,04,000 crore) of last fiscal.

Exchange rate management will likely take a back seat to other priorities such as inflation control, say experts. The RBI has the difficult task of managing very strong capital flows that pose bigger problems for the central bank in liquidity management. Come December, those flows are likely to get even stronger, because of a change in the Morgan Stanley Composite Index (MSCI), which fund managers use for asset allocation to emerging markets. South Korea will be taken off the MSCI, and the result is likely to be an increase in the weight allocated to India. Likely consequence: even stronger inflows.

For textile export firms and other merchandise manufacturers, it seems likely that their industries will undergo a consolidation and restructuring. So corporate India will sooner, rather than later, have to face the question: will the sun set on some of these industries? That said, services exports are not likely to suffer as much. This much seems certain: the exchange rate is likely to stay firm for the next few months. Exporters must now focus on building new competencies rather than clamour for more sops.

A Silver Lining?

Political circles in New Delhi are abuzz not about the prospects of snap polls, but about their timing. Will they be announced immediately after the Budget 2008-09 or after monsoons set in?

Will Left parties use the prospective fuel price hike as the excuse to bring down the UPA government?

General elections trigger demand for certain goods and services across the country. From hiring of auto and man-pulled rickshaws for campaigning to erecting pandals and printing pamphlets, it results in a microconsumption boom at tehsil and district levels. While candidates are required to file expense audits with the Election Commission, party-wise figures are unavailable. For the 2004 general elections, the government budgeted for Rs 800-odd crore on security, expenditure on polling booths, etc. 'It is difficult to say how much parties spend,' says Yashwant Sinha, former finance minister and vice-president of the Bharatiya Janata Party. 'But it is many times the money spent by the government.' Pronab Sen, India's chief statistician, says campaign money adds to GDP growth, but in small measure.

More than the blip in growth rates, it is interesting to notice the change in the economy a political business cycle brings. When a new regime takes charge, it first tries to rein in inflation, for which it adopts contractionary policies that dampen demand. Then, the regime tries to boost demand and fuel growth, simultaneously keeping a tab on prices. In short, the economy derives its up-down cycle every time there is a change in government. Take for example, the Congress-led UPA government, which came to power on the argument that India's growth story was not helping the poor. So, there were schemes such as National Rural Employment Guarantee that fuelled inflation. Monetary tightening followed in the backdrop of rising asset prices and 'overheating' in segments such as construction.

Under-loaded

A slowdown in freight traffic has important implications for overall economic activity. The first signs of a decline in truck rentals along major cross-country routes came in June. According to a report by Indian Foundation of Transport Research and Training (IFTRT), truck rentals declined by as much as 6-10 per cent in the quarter ended 30 June over the same period last year. In the following quarter, rentals along major routes slipped by a further 1.5-3 per cent.

Reason? A decline in cargo offerings from the manufacturing sector, says SP Singh, senior fellow and coordinator at IFTRT. 'For a small trucker, lower cargo availability would mean less round trips for his trucks and, thus, lower earnings.' More disturbingly, in the current quarter, many small truckers have defaulted on auto loan EMIs. 'It is obvious that this would happen considering how both rentals and the number of round trips have declined,' says JL Khanna, joint managing director of Delhi-based Jaipur Golden Transport.

There has been considerable decline in truck sales as well. All categories of trucks, barring 8-12-tonne capacity ones, have declined in sales from 5-21.6 per cent in April-August this year as against the corresponding period last year. 'The decline in sales is largely because of the rise in auto-finance rates,' says M Murali, advisor with All Indian Motor Transport Congress. Singh, however, slams this claim. 'A trucker who has to expand his fleet will not be bothered by a 0.5 per cent rise in interest rates,' he says. Also, most auto companies have been providing discounts ranging from Rs 45,000-Rs 85,000 on various categories of trucks to make up for high interest rates, says Singh.

The only category that has shown a significant rise in sales is the 'tipper', used for moving construction material. With infrastructure development buzzing, this trend is quite predictable. So far, only the small truckers seem to be getting affected, but riding on the back of a sluggish manufacturing sector, the situation might worsen for the bigger truck operators, too.

Interest Rate Blues

The near-unanimous opinion, according to almost everyone BW spoke to, was that interest rates played a considerable role in the

Major trunk routes	Quarterly rental movement		Decline	
	April '07	Sept '07	(Rs)	(%)
Delhi-Chennai-Delhi	75,800	69,000	6,800	8.97
Delhi-Hyderabad-Delhi	56,800	52,000	4,800	8.45
Delhi-Bangalore-Delhi	61,600	56,500	5,100	8.28
Delhi-Kolkata-Delhi	43,600	40,000	3,600	8.26
Delhi-Mumbai-Delhi	38,300	35,800	2,500	6.53
				Source: IFTRT

And the rates came tumbling after ...

cooling off. Where they differed was on whether it was a good thing for the economy at large. Retail credit growth and housing have been the biggest casualties.

With the cut in key policy interest rates by the US Federal Reserve in mid-September, many are suggesting that the RBI should follow suit. This, say industry associations, will spur investment, allow consumption to bounce back, and everybody wins. Which is why the RBI's quarterly review of the monetary policy on 31 October is keenly awaited, not only by companies in sectors that are rate-sensitive, but also by banks, which have seen a sharp slowdown in credit disbursals this year.

If economic indicators are a traffic signal, KV Kamath, managing director and CEO of ICICI Bank, India's second largest bank, says the recent IIP numbers are amber. 'The policy makers will have to take a call on interest rates, as a slowdown (in the growth rate) will make it difficult to regain momentum,' he says. Credit growth has slowed to 23.6 per cent in 2007 compared with 31 per cent as on March-end 2007. According to the RBI's 28 September weekly statistical supplement, bank credit to businesses and consumers was Rs 63,258 crore in this financial year, 40 per cent lower than the Rs 1,05,437 crore during the corresponding period last year.

It is understandable that Kamath is pitching hard for a rate cut, because his bank has built size and scale on the back of a consumer boom. His remarks highlight a broader and more important point: consumption and corporate investment have become much more interest rate sensitive over the past five years, amplifying the impact that central bank policy signals have on day-to-day lives. The total

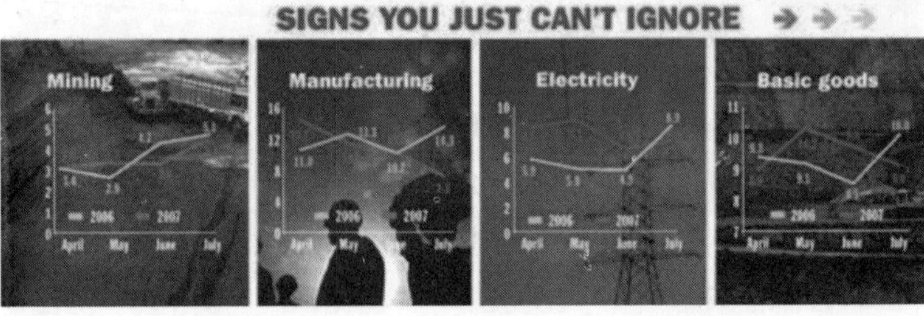

non-food credit extended by banks as a percentage of GDP has more than doubled to 46 per cent now from 21 per cent five years ago. As the charts show (see 'Looming Snags' on page 99), while the hike in reverse repo rates (key lending rate at which the central bank lends to commercial banks) was just 175 basis points since August 2005, the interest rates for companies and retail customers jumped 250 basis points during the same period.

So, are interest rates too high? Monetary tightening through a series of hikes in cash reserve requirements (cash that banks have to park with the RBI, expressed as a percentage of their deposits) to 7 per cent during the last year has jacked up banks' prime lending rate by almost 200 basis points from 11-11.5 per cent in September last to 12.75-13.25 per cent at present. R Sridhar, managing director of Shriram Truck Finance, says higher interest rates have taken a toll on sales of heavy commercial vehicles. 'It has been a 10 per cent dip in case of Tata Motors, the largest truck manufacturer in the country,' he says.

There has been some easing of interest rates, as many banks have cut lending rates for retail credit for auto loans, for instance, and for housing. 'Interest rates have also moderated in the secondary markets,' says the head of fixed income trading at a large securities firm who wished to remain unnamed. 'The one year swap rates have come down by more than 1 per cent from 8.5 per cent to about 7 per cent over the past weeks.' Interest rate swaps allow institutions to hedge themselves against future interest rate changes; a lowering of swap rates implies a moderation in interest rates. Rangarajan himself feels India needs to hold on to its rates. 'We need to wait and watch,' he says, hinting that a rate cut may be thought about only after the third quarter of this financial year.

Besides, it will take 18-24 months for past rate changes to play out in the economy. In its 7 September *India Watch* issue, HSBC

Looming snags

While the RBI hiked repo rates by 175 basis points since August 2005, corporate lending and mortgage interest rates have jumped 250 basis points

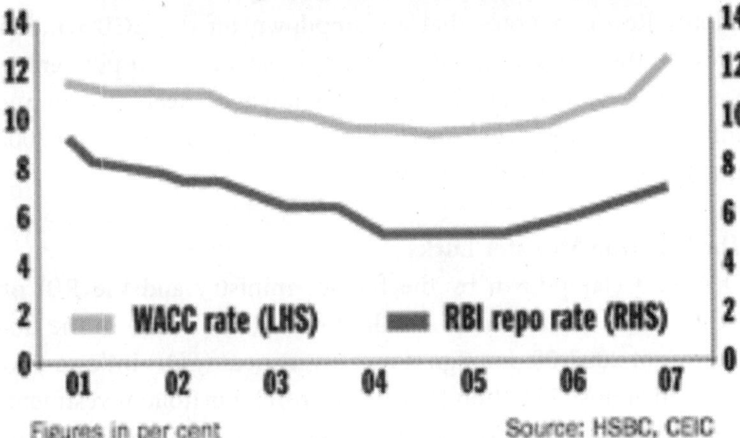

Outstanding credit has more than doubled as a ratio of GDP from 21 per cent in 2002 to 46 per cent now, showing India's rising sensitivity to rate hikes

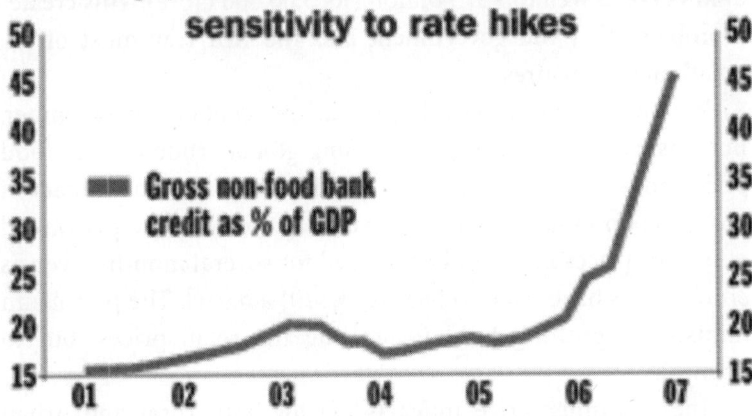

Most IIP indicators have taken a plunge in the past four months

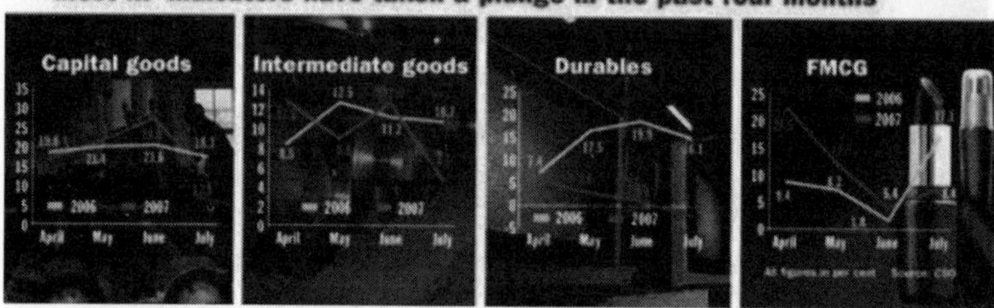

Global Research notes that a clampdown on the ECB window (despite the fact such ECBs account for less than 10 per cent of total bank credit) signalled the RBI's intent to keep growth and inflation in some sort of check. 'It will not be until well into 2008 that these effects are felt,' it says.

The Inflation Monster Lurks

Despite a clampdown by the finance ministry and the RBI on ECBs, India Inc. raised $7.4 billion (Rs 29,600 crore) in the first quarter of 2007-08. Foreign direct investment (FDI) inflows have touched almost $5 billion (Rs 20,000 crore); portfolio investments account for $11.3 billion (Rs 45,200 crore) in April to September, compared with $7.1 billion (Rs 28,400 crore) in the whole of last year. While the PM's Economic Advisory Council estimated total capital flows of $58 billion (Rs 2,32,000 crore) this fiscal, Rangarajan now admits that this figure could be substantially higher: capital inflows could well top $75 billion (Rs 3,00,000 crore). This creates a problem that the government and the RBI fear most of all: inflationary pressures.

Inflation hit its five-year low of 3.23 per cent on 15 September. But this excludes the impact of rising global crude oil and food prices on the wholesale price index. In real terms, the impact of fuel costs on inflation is a negative 2.5 per cent, since petrol and other fuel prices have not been raised for several months, even as crude prices have risen to $83 (Rs 3,320) a barrel. The petroleum ministry is pushing hard for raising the retail prices, but to no avail.

The consumer price index (CPI) for both rural and urban consumers continues to be fairly high. It rose to 7.26 per cent in August from a year earlier, higher than July's annual rise of 6.25 per cent, mainly due to an increase in food prices. The wholesale

EXECUTIVE SUMMARY

- **A slow landing looks certain. What is not certain is whether it could become a precipitous fall**
- **Moderation in interest rates is unlikely because of fears that inflation could raise its ugly head**
- **Surge in capital flows will further strengthen the rupee, dampening export prospects**

price index – which hit a five-year low of 3.23 per cent and is the official inflation number – does not capture consumer and food prices.

And the RBI is unlikely to undertake any steps – like a cut in policy interest rates – that could upset this fragile balance. Besides the risk of inflation, a price hike on diesel or petrol will act like an additional tax on the economy, increasing the cost of production and making the economy more expensive.

So What Happens Now?

In its World Economic Outlook report released in April this year, the International Monetary Fund (IMF) expected the world economy to grow at a slower 4.9 per cent in 2007 and 2008 from 5.4 per cent recorded in 2006. It had revised downwards the growth rate for the US to 2.2 per cent against its own September 2006 estimate of 2.9 per cent. In 2006, US GDP grew 3.3 per cent. IMF's estimates of India growth rates for 2007 and 2008 are 8.4 per cent and 7.8 per cent, respectively. The IMF has now said it will revise world growth rates further downwards. India, being an economy largely driven by domestic demand, and its share in global trade being just about 1 per cent, may not be much affected due to changes in the advanced economies. However, a recession in the US could drive growth rates down to 7 per cent, according to some.

The economic news could get a little more worrisome. While corporate profits are expected to be robust, niggling doubts are emerging. 'Although business confidence in India is still at elevated levels, sentiment and expectations appear to be softening,' says

Ruth Stroppiana, director of Asia Pacific at Moody's Economy.com, a subsidiary of Moody's Corporation. 'There could be some easing in companies' investment and hiring plans in the next six months or so,' she says. In a recent paper titled 'The Elephant's charge expected to slow', Stroppiana estimated India's growth rate to be between 7 per cent and 8 per cent during 2007-11.

That said, domestic demand is expected to pick up in the festival season, so we may see an uptick in growth, albeit a marginal one. But the aspirations of hitting double-digit growth in the next year appear unrealistic. 'That would lead to overheating in the economy, something we have come close to,' says Indranil Pan, chief economist of Kotak Mahindra Bank. For right now, let's all take a breather.

Punya Prasun Bajpai

Punya Prasun Bajpai, 44, is Consulting Editor, Zee News. Bajpai won this award for his story published in the Hindi weekly magazine, *Pratham Pravakta*.

[Women were being raped and young men were dragged out of their houses and labeled Naxals, then killed by the police. But their struggle was all about securing sustainability for themselves.]

INNUMERABLE ENCOUNTERS: DOOMED TRIBALS

Award-winning Story

This is a story of police brutality where incidents of rape of tribal women do not stir the psyche. Blamed of helping the Naxalites, the local police enjoy the opportunity to kill these poor folks, randomly. The state government has accepted what the police calls 'encounter' which has taken the lives of two thousand tribal people in one year. Fifty tribal people were killed in Chhattisgarh last year alone, by security forces. Twenty-one tribal women suffered the trauma of gang rape. Six were killed after rape. Two of them were pregnant. While fake encounters in Gujarat are hitting the national headlines, the horrendous treatment the tribals get in Chhattisgarh goes unreported.

A state like Chhattisgarh has become hellish for its inhabitants. The contrast between the lush dreams of development and the dark state of common farmers is quite scary. The mad rush of industrialisation has not only destroyed the ecology, but also degraded tribal life. Much of the tribal population has migrated to big cities and is working as labourers for multi-storey buildings. The exploitation and suffering of these tribals fail to grab the attention of even the local newspapers.

The Chhattisgarh government treats this land as a breeding ground for terror. It accuses the tribals of subscribing to the Naxal ideology, something the state cannot tolerate.

In a small village in Surguja district of Chhattisgarh, the police arrested a tribal woman Ledha, also known as Seema. According to the police she was the main culprit behind the March 2006 bomb blast in which three CISF men lost their lives. Seema was pregnant when she was picked up by the cops in April 2006. Seema's husband Ramesh Nageshia had links with Maoists. The court sentenced Seema to one-and-a-half years of imprisonment. Seema gave birth to a very weak baby in the jail. Later, the court acquitted Seema saying the case against her was weak. Seema or Ledha was free of the slur of being a Naxalite, but the police pressurised Ledha. It convinced her husband to surrender. They lured her by promising job and money. Ledha persuaded her husband for the sake of their son to surrender so that they could enjoy a better life. It was decided that Ramesh would surrender at the house of the secretary Civildah Gram Panchayat, on 28 March 2006.

The superintendent of police of Surguja, CRP Kalauri reached Civildah with Ledha. An additional force from Kusumi came with him. As soon as the police reached the place, they started thrashing Ramesh. He was beaten so brutally that his body turned blue and then suddenly the assistant platoon commander of the Special Armed Forces put the pistol to his temple and shot him. Ramesh died on the spot. Ledha was so shocked that she could not even scream out her grief. She just shivered. Then she was taken to the Shankargarh police station and warned not to say anything about the incident otherwise she would face the same fate. Ledha kept quiet. After three months, on Dussehra, the police again picked up Ledha with her old father and brought them to the police station, where she was stripped in the presence of SP Kallauri and raped in front of her father. For the next ten days she was kept in the lock-up and was repeatedly sexually assaulted by the cops. During this her old father was kept in another lock-up. But her weak son, unable to speak, was with her and witnessed her ordeal. Despite all this Ledha did not die. She is still alive and has reached the Chhattisgarh High Court with her case. In January 2007, Bilaspur High Court filed the case. In the first hearing the public prosecutor argued that Ledha was lying.

This is the first case which has reached the courtroom. There are many other tribal women who have faced even worse monstrosities in the last year. Though Ledha is alive, many others have lost their lives. There are six cases registered at the police station in which women were killed after being gang-raped: Sukki and Kursum Lakke of Peddakorma village, Vedinje Mulli and Vedinje Naggi of Mookavalli village. Boogam Somvari of Kotaloo and Midkaam Sunny of Etepad village were first raped and then murdered. Mudkaam Sunny and Vedinje Naggi were pregnant when they were sexually assaulted.

Furthermore, these women are pawns in the hands of tendu leaf contractors and serve as informers throughout the area. As these contractors make big bucks selling the tendu-leaves, they provide a channel of information to the security personnel about the Naxal operations. In cases when the contractors feel that the tribal labourers are asking for too much money for collecting tendu leaves, they accuse the tribal women of being connected with Naxalites. The police intervene and the women are brutalised, sometimes even slaughtered.

From July to October 2006, more than 50 tribals were killed by the security forces. Dozens of tribal women were raped, villages were put to flame. Cattle were slaughtered. There seems to be a conspiracy at work. One end is the contractor who leaves the tribal people at the mercy of the security forces and the other end is the government whose developmental rush is devouring the lands of tribal inhabitants.

Apart from the 54 tribals shot by police, Mankewal Munder, Alboor, Polttayam, Mazzimedari, Pullum and Chinnakorama are a few villages where more then 250 tribal people are missing. The names of 128 villagers among them are listed in the different government welfare projects. The allotted money is reaching their homes on paper, surprisingly, duly signed by them. Nobody knows where they are.

The way the security personnel maintain law and order is nothing short of farcical. On 21 July houses of two farmers were burnt down in Pondum village; Pallewala village was looted and vandalised. Ten persons including three tribal women were arrested.

22 July: Munder village. Cattle were slaughtered or taken away by policemen; 10 houses set aflame. The villagers left this village and took shelter in the neighbouring village, Phoolgutta.

25 July: Phoolgutta became the police target – 50 tribals were taken to the police station.

29 July: the security forces hit Karrebodhali village – people were thrashed. And 15 tribals were arrested.

12 August: 2 farmers of Katloor village were trapped at Kutaroo market. Later, their cases were filed up as encounters.

15 August: houses of 5 farmers at Jangla village were razed down by tendu leaf contractor. The contractor took shelter at the local police station. No FIR was filed against him. Instead, a fake story that villagers of Jangla had a link with the Naxalites was registered.

The tales go on and on.

At the other end of the spectrum is the government's modernisation drive to improve the so-called law and order situation in the state. For example, Rs 700 crore was allotted for vehicles and weapons; Rs 1,200 crore was set aside to construct good stretches of roads. To build strong walls at police stations and to construct police guest houses, the government agreed to give Rs 150 crore. On the other hand, to provide the minimum food grain to every tribal, according to the government's own calculations, required Rs 100 crore. But that is possible only if the police, the administration, gram panchayat, MLAs, MPs spare the amount.

Chhattisgarh is rich in natural resources: 90 per cent of India's tin is here, 16 per cent coal, 19 per cent iron ore, 50 per cent of India's diamonds are found here. Overall, 28 per cent of our mineral wealth is found in the state. But such is the level of corruption in the state that the tribals do not profit from this wealth which is exploited in the name of development to earn more from exports. From central security forces to police stations, collector to MLAs, everybody is devouring money allotted for different welfare causes.

This can easily be understood by looking at the profile of the projects of national or foreign companies. The state government has signed a Memorandum of Understanding (MoU) to start a plant to produce 1000 megawatt electricity with the American company Texas Power Generation. The state will get Rs 20 lakh dollars for this. Another American company, One Incorporate, has finalised a deal to open a medicine factory worth Rs 50 crore. Chhattisgarh Electricity Board has made a deal with IFCO (Indian Farmers Cooperative Limited) to establish a plant worth Rs 5 crore to to produce 1000 megawatts of electricity at Surguja. In this deal, the state has got 26 per cent of the shares and the other 74 per cent will go to IFCO. At a time when everybody is talking about the privatisation of electricity, plants like these may be sold to some multinational companies for 10,000 crore. The Tata Group is going to establish a steel plant in Bastar at the cost of Rs 7,000 crore with the aid from the World Bank. ESSAR has also agreed to fund a caustic power plant worth Rs 4,000 crore. Prakash Sponge Iron Limited is interested in coal mines in Korba. Apart from this, there are dozens of multinational companies interested in harnessing the rich natural resources of this land and will not hesitate in spending thousands of crores.

How big deals are finalised for meagre sums can easily be seen in the case of Bailadila. The iron which is taken out from Bailadila mines is sold to Japan at Rs 160/ tonne (16 p/kilo). The same iron is sold to other companies for the industries in Mumbai at Rs 450/ tonne and to the industrialists of Chhattisgarh at Rs 1600/tonne. The presence of Nagamar Steel Plant, Tisco, ESSAR Pipeline project (to send iron-powder to Japan from Bailadila through water) will adversely impact the existing water resource of Bastar. Already, farmers do not have enough water to irrigate their land. Fields and crops are ruined. Farmers are committing suicide or leaving behind their natural habitat for the city to work as labourers at construction sites, or to work as cheap labour at brick-kilns.

If the government sanctions all these projects, 60 per cent of the agricultural land will be lost. It also means that without Special Economic Zone(s) (SEZ) 50,000 acres of land will be under the control of multinational companies and about a lakh of tribal farmers will lose their land.

Meetings called by the central government to discuss the status of this tribal populated area, have been dominated by concerns about internal security in this Naxal affected area, the condition of the security force posted there, and the need to modernise their weapons. In all the Naxal affected areas in nine states which are below the poverty line, the stress is on building basic infrastructure. The chief ministers of these states raised the question of development and mentioned the difficulties multinational companies face in commuting and sought help from the centre. At every level it is unanimously agreed that there will be no compromise on the issue of development and establishing industries. Thus, there will be beautiful roads, well-lit areas for the companies.

There was not a single mention of the tribals, of women like Ledha who were raped and killed brutally. At no level have questions been raised about the violence in the tribal populated areas or the culture of fake encounters. The state government is supposed to answer such questions. If the state defends itself by saying that it did not know about police terror then it is a dangerous symptom. This is not merely a matter of killing tribal people in fake encounters or strengthening the internal security on account of Naxalite activities, but it is alarming for our democracy, which is being used as a disguise by the administration to create terror.

RAVIK BHATTACHARYA

Ravik Bhattacharya, 30, is Principal Correspondent, *The Indian Express*.

[Visits to the villages involved in the Nandigram clashes brought out tales of the gruesome atrocities committed by the state's forces and the Opposition.]

NIGHT WITHOUT END

Award-winning Story

At the Nandigram Block Hospital, the eerie silence is broken by the groans of the injured. Then there is a scream which peters out. Another death?

It's midnight. A medical staffer walks up to the hospital gate where anxious villagers stand in a huddle and says something. Basudeb Purwa, a supporter of the Bhoomi Uchched Protirodh Committee (BUPC), which has been at the receiving end of the CPM cadres' wrath for the past week, turns around and smiles. His wife Sabita has given birth to a girl. 'Sir, it is a girl. My first baby,' beams Purwa. It's the first good news he has heard in months. A moment of hope in times of despair. But it's a moment, just that. For, he can't shake off the terror that has gripped him. 'The CPM men beat up my family members and ransacked my house because we took part in the BUPC rally,' says Purwa. The violence came at a time his wife was going into labour, but the primary health centre near their village had been shut for 11 months. 'I put her on a rickshaw van when they attacked my village. The CPM cadres stopped us to check a number of times. I implored them to let us through,' says Purwa. His wife gave birth in the women's ward, alongside women injured in the violence that has torn Nandigram apart in the past fortnight, with the CPM taking on supporters of the BUPC, the group which is protesting against the government's acquisition of land. Bhaktipada Das, among those outside the hospital, is also a proud father of a baby boy born in the evening. 'My wife and child are fine,' he smiles. It's Tuesday night and it has been three hours since we decided to travel through the night in a Nandigram where nowadays, the day is as dark as the night, a Nandigram still smarting from the violence unleashed by the CPM activists, adamant on recapturing their fiefdom that they had lost to the protesters. The land being protected by the protesters led by BPUC has been acquired for a chemical hub by the West Bengal government under the SEZ policy. In March, clashes between the police and the people took over 14 lives. Since then, there has been simmering tension in Nandigram, but CPM supporters had to leave the town alone. That is until last week, when armed communist activists attacked the people and regained lost ground. The moon is visible; so are thousands of stars on this clear winter night (electricity supply is erratic in these parts). This is our night journey in Nandigram.

9.30 p.m. Nandigram Town: Men of the Central Reserve Police Force (CRPF) are positioned at major crossings; others patrol the streets. The roads empty out and even the crowd outside the police station, the busiest spot here for the past 11 months, disperses. RP Singh, a CRPF officer out with his men, says they have been here for just two days. 'The town shuts down early here,' says Singh, comparing it with the industrial town of Dhanbad where they were stationed. 'We are doing our duty. Reassuring the people is most vital and our men are doing their best. We will patrol all night so that the people can sleep,' he adds.

9.45 p.m.: The state electricity board does its bit to put people to sleep with a blackout. It's the third power failure this evening but the shopkeepers and food-stall owners aren't overly disturbed. Within minutes, candles and lanterns are taken out and lit.

10 p.m.: A teashop near the Nandigram police station is pulling its shutters down for the day, the last in the area to do so. Owner Harihar rinses the cups and the kettle while some hangers-on talk in hushed tones of the deprivations of the past 11 months, the horrors of the past few days and a dread of the future. 'Hundreds of people died, bodies were thrown into the river,' they say, 'as armed cadres attacked villages. Now the CPM is in charge and we have been told to join their rallies. What do we do? We have to think of our lives first,' says one of the teashop regulars, Zulfikar Ali. 'Armed cadres are openly doing the rounds on bikes,' he says. Harihar's shop is the only one in the neighbourhood that remains open so late. 'I keep it open till late because of the police station nearby. Business has been good for

the past 11 months. So many people come here, so many policemen. They like my tea,' he says.

11 p.m.: We are the only civilians on the roads. We head off for the relief camp at Brajamohan Tiwari School at one end of Nandigram town. The school is now a camp for thousands of people from neighbouring villages seeking shelter from the CPM marauders. The sickly smell of fear and waste clings to the school. A few halogen lights break the darkness. On the school ground, hundreds queue up for their relief 'dinner'. Most have plastic packets in their hands; the lucky ones have sal-leaf plates. 'When armed CPM cadres set fire to my house in Saudkhali, I managed to save my two children but nothing else. Now we have nothing,' says Sabita Jana, a housewife. Volunteers dole out a few ladles of rice, dal and vegetables. Even women with newborn children wait their turn. The men sit inside the classrooms, desultorily having their dinner. Again, the women wait their turn. There are no Hindus and Muslims here. No upper caste or lower caste. They are all refugees. The sleeping arrangements are simple: women and children sleep inside the classrooms, the men outside. Four armed guards man the locked gates but their number seems inadequate. 'Armed CPM activists sometimes come and threaten us even here,' adds Jana. 'I could not find my husband. My elder son went missing when CPM men fired on a peace *michil* (rally) a few days ago. I found him yesterday in Nandigram hospital; he can barely speak. Shyamal – my boy – is just fifteen years old.' Most women here haven't been able to trace their husbands and relatives. A non-governmental organisation has brought a medical team but their number is hopelessly outmatched by that of the injured and the ill. Bhabani Das, a leader of the BUPC, says: 'It is very hard to arrange food, shelter and protection for so many people. Some are returning home to face the inhuman atrocities. It is especially hard for women and children.' At the Block Hospital, we meet with life. And walk on.

1 a.m.: Nandigram police station: A couple of jeeps drive out with CRPF men and a police guide, leaving the station almost deserted. Behind the lone sentry is the sub-inspector on night duty, Pradyut Ghosh. 'Everyone is so tired, they've all gone to sleep. For the past 11 months, we have been on strict duty. All leave was cancelled. Now we have to take care of the CRPF. The streams of

VIPs, netas also take their toll on us,' says Ghosh. The silver lining? The lock-ups are empty. 'No usual complaints of thefts or anything,' says the SI.

2 a.m. Maheshpur Bazaar: Enveloped in winter mist, the streets are deserted; stray dogs bark their annoyance. All doors are bolted. The few villagers who are still out, melt away when they see the Express car. A lone figure emerges from behind a row of shops, torch in hand. Introductions over, he gives a signal and fifteen people come out of the dark. They are all night guards who, for the last 11 months, had taken turns to patrol the area. By day they are shopkeepers and villagers. 'Some of us returned two days ago after the BUPC went away. Today the CPM rules here and everything is peaceful. We are guarding against the BUPC people,' says one. 'Political allegiance does not matter, our homes and shops do,' says another. 'Now things are peaceful, but there is fear in the air. We have seen people being shot dead and houses burnt down. We try and save whoever or whatever we can,' says Shankar Parul, a shopkeeper-cum-night guard. A final word of caution: 'No one will speak to you here.' And it is not safe for us to be here, we are told. We move on.

2.30 a.m. Tekhali Bridge: Bordering Nandigram and Khejuri, the bridge demarcates the strongholds of the BUPC and the CPM. Tonight, dressed in red flags, the bridge stands deserted. The sandbag bunkers, once used by the police, are unmanned. Neither the CRPF nor the Eastern Frontier Rifles which has a camp nearby, are present on the bridge.

3 a.m.: Maheshpur High School: Our car is stopped by a group of lathi-wielding CPM youths. Eight men with flags and lathis greet us and ask us a number of questions and check our credentials. 'We take turns to watch the area. You never know when the BUPC people might retaliate,' says Manu Das, fish vendor and party cadre, almost apologetically. 'We have formed a village rakskhi bahini and the BUPC and outsiders are not allowed. Which side are you on?' asks Das. Further down, we meet Swapan Das, a CPM supporter who says he was chased from the village by Trinamool Congress adherents heading the protest against land acquisition in February and has only now managed to return home. 'The Trinamool people burnt down my house in February and I fled along with my wife and children. They committed atrocities, beat

up people and raped girls. We have spent 11 months in the Khejuri camp in inhuman conditions. My food stall was ransacked and my two bigha land remained untilled. Now it is our turn,' says Das, who returned home last Wednesday. Manu Das, the fish vendor, also talks revenge. 'We have a list of neighbours who will not be allowed to come back. Their property belongs to us now. If they try to return, they will be finished.' CPM cadres tell us that they are opening the schools closed for months. Women feel safer now, they claim.

3.30 a.m.: A tea stall: Near Hospital More crossing is the first to open. The owner, seventy-eight-year-old Lakshmikanta Jana, begins his early morning routine. 'For the past 11 months, fear and bloodshed have ruled the area. But business was good. I am the first to open at 2.30 a.m. every day. People have thronged the hospital and many of them depend on me for their tea and bread,' says Jana. He has been running this shop for the past twenty-two years. 'Never have I seen such trouble in Nandigram. This was a very peaceful area until Buddhadeb (Bhattacharjee, the West Bengal chief minister) decided to take our land,' he says. 'Whenever there was firing and bombing in the area, I closed my shop. Four days ago, when the CPM men came on motorcycles, there was a lot of trouble. They sprayed bullets on the walls,' he adds. The night was dark, but the rising sun does not appear to dispel the darker days in Nandigram.

LIFE IN THE MIDST OF DEATH

Personal Account

One of the finest and most memorable moments of my Nandigram coverage was a night when I was overwhelmed by an event that came as a big surprise but with a sense of joy, too. It was one night when I and photographer, Subham Dutta decided to keep awake and move around to see Nandigram by night. Days here used to be filled with action and arson, firing and fights between rival outfits. We were often caught in the middle. We had witnessed, first hand, innumerable days filled with bloodshed and violence. But life in Nandigram after nightfall was an unknown territory for us. And we decided to give it a try.

The first hurdle came from our Tata Sumo driver who would not sit behind the steering wheel whatever be the remuneration. Life is more precious than money, he told us.

'Sahib, you cannot move in an area at dead of night where even day time travel is not safe. How can you request me to take you around Nandigram through the night?' Manoj, the driver asked.

'There are bullets, sir. I cannot drive if you want to die, go ahead. I will not go to my death, knowingly,' was Manoj's forceful pleas. We fully shared his apprehensions but the call of the unknown somehow egged us on. We finally managed to persuade him and set out for a night in Nandigram.

At about midnight we stopped at Nandigram block hospital. The groans of some injured persons broke the night's silence. There was also a huddle of people outside the hospital, their faces animated in the flicker of light reflected out of the hospital windows. We decided to take a look inside, expecting fresh arrivals of the injured or bodies from the interiors of Nandigram, the usual scenario. No, not this time.

Amidst the injured and the dead, we saw a group of villagers beaming with joy. Basudeb Purwa, a supporter of the Bhoomi Uchched Protirodh Committee (BUPC – Save the Land Committee), which had been at the receiving end of the CPI(M) cadres' wrath for the past week, turned around and smiled at us.

'My wife, Sabita has given birth to a baby,' Purwa said.

'Sir, it's a girl. My first baby,' said Purwa.

In the midst of the months of violence in Nandigram, where corpses and injured were the only happenings for us in days, the birth of a baby was more than a welcome break. The gloom of that night immediately changed as we shared that moment of hope in times of despair not only for the Purwa family but also for us. We shared every bit of joy along with the assembled crowd.

'The CPI(M) men had beaten up my family members and ransacked my house because we had participated in a rally organized by the Committee to Protect Land and Eviction,' said Purwa. The trouble started when his wife was going into labour. The primary health centre near their village had been shut for eleven months.

'I put her on a rickshaw van when the CPM men attacked our village. The CPM cadres stopped us to check a number of times. I managed to persuade them to allow our passage,' says Purwa. Alongside Sabita and her baby, in the hospital, were injured women from different parts of Nandigram.

But the feeling of joy evaporated as soon as we drove deep into the villages, well past midnight. The silence of the night was occasionally shattered by the sound of bombs or explosives.

We stopped and got down near an open field that during the day served as a marketplace. As we parked our vehicle, the desolate, dark field suddenly came alive with life, with over 200 men emerging from the shadows and virtually encircling us.

'We are here as night sentry. Who are you and on which side do you belong? What are you doing here at this hour?' one of the youth in the mob asked as he began to frisk us before we could reply.

After a prolonged conversation we were able to convince the youths that we were reporters and did not have any political bias. We wanted to see Nandigram by night, we told them. Once convinced, the CPI(M) cadres came clean. They were CPI(M) cadres who had regained their lost turf after being driven out by the BUPC.

We realized that the nights in Nandigram are as volatile as days. There are watchful eyes behind the void and nightly silence, there are battles over territory and battles over political loyalty.

[illegible] wanted [illegible] indigenously might [illegible] them. [illegible] [illegible] CRIRC [illegible] came [illegible]. The [illegible] and [illegible] for [illegible] the BCCI.

[illegible] said that the Muslims or Naxalites are [illegible]. There [illegible] behind the [illegible] are [illegible] territory and [illegible] over political [illegible].

Rudraneil Sengupta

Rudraneil Sengupta, 29, is Features Writer with *Mint*. He worked for CNN-IBN when he went to cover a rafting competition.

[In a cricket crazy nation, Rudraneil Sengupta brought into focus the joy of rafting at the National Rafting Championship despite its inherent dangers.]

RAFTING ON THE ROOFTOP OF THE WORLD

Personal Account

Leh's central square is buzzing. The narrow, undulating streets that converge into the town centre bring rafters and river guides, all heading for the Al-Fresco Café that basks in the glittering Ladakh sun. Cries of 'Juley, Juley' – (the one-stop Ladakhi word for hello, goodbye, how are you, I'm good) – rings out in every corner.

I'm in high country, covering the National Rafting Championship, and today is rendezvous day. Rafters from all over India, bitten by the charm of Ladakh, and high on the oxygen-depleted air at over 11,000 feet, are bouncing with joy and excitement.

'The rooftop of the world!'

'Juley!'

'Juley, juley!'

'Where's Riju?'

'Call Thinley!'

'Juley!'

'Mint tea for everyone? It's the specialty here – it'll get you warm to the bone!'

'There's Shankar – Juley!'

Laughter and warmth spill out onto the main street; rafting teams, organisers, judges, safety personnel, drivers, and porters discuss logistics over steaming glasses of mint tea. The competition will begin next morning. My cameraperson, Suraj, and I sit through this meeting to understand how events will unfold over the next few days, pitching in with our own concerns, soaking in the fun-loving, testosterone-fuelled world of river-guides.

Our one-point person is Manishankar Ghosh – a large man with a Buddha-like face, narrow eyes, and a mouth that can go

Rafters from all over India come to Ladakh to participate in the National Rafting championship.

from severe to a wide, uninhibited, luminous smile in a fraction of a second. One look at him and you know you are in safe hands. He's been running rivers for almost twenty years now – he's seen it all! Mani listens patiently as I explain the logistics of the shoot. He doesn't blink when I tell him that we shoot an average six hours of footage for a half-hour show. I explain the different angles we would need for the shoot. We needed to be extra careful with the handling of the camera. Mani assigns us a car that would race ahead of the rafts and get us to position for good shots of the approaching rafts.

Large parts of the competition will be in the spectacular gorge cut through by the Zanskar river – steep cliff sides that rise straight out of the churning water, severely limiting the number of places we can access by the river to shoot the boats. The road is too high to get any meaningful shots. It's a logistical nightmare. Mani is happy, it's a challenge. He assures us he will be with us throughout. Meanwhile, Suraj and I are saying our prayers.

Next morning, Mani arrives in a jeep and takes us on a recce of the competition area. We drive to the point from where the rafts will start the race – there's a wide riverbank, ideal for a shoot. Once that's done, we'll have to race ahead of the rafts and arrive at a wooden footbridge that spans the river. It's flimsy and beautiful, like a bridge to a lost civilization. We get a lovely overhead shot from here – a bird's eye view. But once the boats cross the bridge, we have to rush back to the car and race ahead again. This time Mani brings us to a part of the road where the slope to the river is gentler than the usual near-vertical drop. It's still hair-raising though and Suraj and I clamber down with our equipment, while Mani times us with a military commander's look. I can see he is enjoying our boot-camp training. From here, we climb up again to the road, heavy camera equipment impeding us at every step – dragging us down, putting us off balance, while chunks of loose rock slip from under our feet and avalanche towards the river.

The next shooting point is another slope where the gradient is manageable, but even steeper than the first. We go down almost in a snowboard move, in a sideways slide with knees bent to keep balance and ankles stuck firmly in the slipping gravel. Going back up is not an option without rope safety, so Mani suggests that the rescue raft pick us up from the riverside and we do the rest of the shoot from inside the raft – which we needed to do anyway.

The morning of the competition is crisp and clear. We drive out towards the competition stretch of the river, past breathtaking

The site of the large part of the competition is the spectacular gorge cut through by the Zanskar river.

The temperature of water – 3° to 5° C – in Zanskar makes the adventure thrilling!

natural beauty. Suraj is shooting without pause; he can't get enough of it. Tall wild grass glows an unreal green under a glacial blue sky, white flowers break like surf over a green sea of grass. Sometimes on the steep sides of the cliffs, a monastery appears etched in the stone – you might miss them, pass them over as rocky outcrop if it wasn't for the tell-tale rows of blackened windows, and sometimes the glimpse of bright prayer flags fluttering in the wind.

I have Riju Raj Singh in the car with me – a handsome man with a charming smile that can melt glaciers, a high-profile lawyer in Delhi, but a river-guide and mountain-man in every bone of his body. Riju is talking me through the nitty-gritty of river-rescue, telling me of the time when a bus had fallen into the river near Manali and how he and his friends loaded their vehicle with rafts and went straight into rescue-mode.

'We saw the bus in the river, half-submerged on its side. It was stuck in a wide rapid, groaning like a metal beast with the push and pull of the river. Hundreds of people and policemen watched helplessly from the road. Even as we looked for a route to get our rafts down to the river, we saw a man sucked out from under the bus and swept away. He looked like a rag doll, taken by the river with no resistance at all. We were stunned, you could hear the gasp from the crowd over the roar of the river. There was no time at all. We scrambled down with the rafts somehow, used a long rope to anchor our boat to a rock and caught an eddy. You know what an eddy is? These are basically upriver currents that occur for short stretches near the riverbanks. What you can do with an eddy is to get the boat into the upstream flow and go till the end of the eddy and steer out of it to catch the main downriver flow. That's what we did. We caught the eddy, went up to the bus, pulled out as many people as we could before the main current pushed us away. We must have made five or six trips before it got completely dark. It was a strange feeling afterwards: we felt good, an adrenaline rush because we managed to save so many people but about half the people in that bus died as well. It was still a tragedy.'

By the end of his story, we are at the starting point of the race. I am introduced to the rescue team – a quiet, efficient and ever-smiling group of young boys who love getting their pictures taken. They are kayakers, the men who turn into fish when they slip inside their brightly coloured, perfectly aerodynamic kayaks. They perform their tricks for the camera, rolling into the river and resurfacing, scooting like water insects in and out of rapids and rocks at breathtaking speed. Watching them, my fears of the river start to fade away. Most of the kayakers I meet are young boys from Nepal, itinerant, illiterate, charming men who've made the mountain rivers of India and Nepal their playground

There is a perception that an adventure sport is a white man's game. That's only partly true. In countries like New Zealand, Canada, United Kingdom, Germany and France, adventure sports have an avid following. In India, it leads an almost invisible existence. That's not for want of talent or interest though. Scattered across the whole of India's vast mountain regions, there are thousands of brilliant kayakers, fearless climbers, and fabulous skiers. But they are all backroom boys. There's no funding or system to support competitive adventure sports or expeditions, and there is no culture of competition either. So all our skiers and climbers and kayakers work for the tourism industry, teach or get hired as guides and expedition support staff. There are exceptions: individuals who made money in tourism and then funded themselves to compete abroad. Those like Tenzing Norgay, part of one of the most mythical quests, were lucky to be partnered with sensitive humanists like Sir Edmund Hillary. By and large, guides and porters go unnoticed and unheralded, whether or not they reach the summit first, or drag the rest of the team to the summit single-handedly.

The kayakers who travel with us are highly skilled and immensely playful, like Brazilian footballers. They are attached to the river with an umbilical cord. The moment they get into the freezing water, they go into a frenzy of acrobatic stunts. They turn turtle; they flip the kayak on its belly, they are upside down under the water, then they roll upright again (the most important kayaking skill – the Eskimo roll!). Just imagine – it's like you are driving a car, and it flips on its roof, and you hit a switch, and the car turns upright! That's what James Bond does. These guys don't have a switch; they just use their core muscles. One of them goes headlong towards a rapid, catching the upturned hood of a wave to execute a somersault. Where have I seen this before? This muscular grace and beauty in the water? This complete mastery of the waves and currents? Oh yes, dolphins on the National Geographic channel! These boys are tougher than teak. They are lean and small, but they can carry abnormally heavy luggage. They run up and down steep mountain paths any number of times without fatigue. They eat little, because they eat last, and inevitably get half their share at the common lunches. Who can stop them if they were trained for competition?

We are on the river now. Suraj has his camera wrapped in layers of cling-film and bubble wrap – he has just enough space to operate the camera – a carabiner and line are attached to the camera and anchored to the raft. The rapids on the Zanskar are high and fast, and the water muddy and opaque. The rush is incredible: one moment I'm floating gently down the stark golden cliffs, staring wonder-eyed at the brilliant designs etched on the rocks by thousands of years of wind and water; the next minute I'm bracing myself to hit a frothing rapid hard, fast, and head-on. My heart is racing, cortisol slows down my brain and I see things in slow-motion as the raft crashes against a wave, rides over it, is pushed ten feet sideways by a current, lifted up by another wave and dropped again. All this while the icy water is incessantly whip-lashing us, and we are paddling furiously, our guide shouting 'forward, forward' to keep us going. Every time the water hits me, my whole body goes into shock, my hands shiver and my fingers feel so numb that I can hardly hold on to the paddle. It's my guide's voice that keeps me together, keeps me going. And surprise, surprise, when we come out of the rapid, I'm raring to hit the next one. By now it's clear to me what makes the Zanskar so dangerous, and by the warped logic of adventure, so thrilling – it's the temperature of the water.

On an average, the water is between three and five degrees celsius and since water conducts heat away from the body about 25 times faster than air, falling into this water is flirting with death. It takes about 15 minutes before hypothermia sets in and if you are not out of the water by then, death is a mere ten minutes away. That's why rescue here is a precision art, executed at deadly speed. 'Jump in and see for yourself what it feels like,' my guide tells me, 'it's the only way to understand the river, it's absolutely necessary if you want to raft or kayak here.' So with a deep breath, steady nerves in I go with an awkward splash. The first minute is not bad, almost invigorating in a disconcerting way as I float downstream in the ice-bath. But almost immediately afterwards, as I begin swimming against the flow towards the raft, the muscles in my feet begin cramping in a painful, helpless way, my arms feel useless and lethargic, and I'm gasping for breath. I keep calm, trying to breath as evenly as I can, thrashing away in slow, ineffectual movements. I watch our young kayaker scoot towards me in a swift, gliding motion. I grab the front of the kayak with both hands, painfully hoisting my legs up to hook them to the side of the kayak (like a sloth bear hanging onto a tree). As soon as I'm secure, the kayak effortlessly turns around and quickly heads back to the boat where I'm hoisted up like a deadweight, cold and shivering. The whole operation lasts just a shade less than 5 minutes, but I'm already a wreck. I sit on the raft, numbed with cold, shivering in uncontrolled spurts of violence. The bright sun, shining uninterrupted by clouds, never felt this good. My guide, Mani, the kayakers, are all proud of me – they grin widely, pat me on the back and it feels great, this joy of crossing a threshold and coming out unharmed. At the next rapid, when the waves lash us, my body is ready for it. I feel like I've taken a giant leap.

As we approach a rapid known to toss boats like confetti at a festival, our guide tells us of a rescue he was involved in at that spot. A fifteen-year-old Italian girl had been pulled in by a large whirlpool at the side of the rapid, right under a sheer cliff-face, after her raft had overturned. Biru was the rescue kayaker for the group, 'I kept my kayak as close to the whirlpool as I could. I was paddling so hard to stay in one place I thought my hands would rip off my shoulders. While doing this, I somehow managed to throw the rescue line at the girl. She was very brave – she just went round and round and did not panic. I was panicking inside my head. My heart was racing. But I still threw the line, she grabbed it and next thing I know, the whirlpool had sucked me in as well. I was upside down in the water, going round and round. There was nothing to do but to bail out of the kayak. So, there we were then – the girl going round and round, me circling a few feet away, the kayak in its own orbit, all of us looking like helpless hens – it was comical, except that we could have died!' He tells me they had to bring in a raft close to the wall, hammer in iron hoops, pass a heavy-duty rope through the iron and then use that as a rescue line. It took the combined force of eight men on the raft to pull them out one by one. It took almost an hour for the rescue. The only reason why they survived was because the water wasn't that cold that day, and everyone was in wet-suits.

With this ominous story, Biru swiftly pulls ahead to show us the way through the rapid – and then it comes to view. A small rapid, just about 20 feet long, but a muscular one, thrashing and roaring, shooting up six feet in the air. We hit the rapid hard, trying to ride over the wave, but we don't hit it hard enough. In a moment that flashes past too fast for my brain to comprehend, the raft overturns and I smash into the water like an arrow. The cold water quickly steadies my brain, and in the underwater chaos, I can see my paddle getting sucked in by the same whirlpool I had just heard about. I lash out with my feet to get away from it and after two or three desperate moves, I am suddenly flung out by the current – I resurface in a tumultuous wave, gulp a mouthful of water instead of air, and then I'm pulled back in, and swept through by the maelstrom. When I surface a few seconds later, I see Biru right beside me – 'Relax,' he says, in a voice very, very calm, 'swim'. I begin swimming, almost like a machine being switched on. It's very hard to swim. I keep feeling like I need to stop and let the current take me wherever. 'Swim,' Biru's monotone cuts through every few seconds. Every time he says it, it strengthens my resolve to swim, till I finally limp on to the shore. I realise later, that in moments of great panic and stress when your brain slows down and almost shuts off, these single, repetitive commands keep you alive. Later in Leh, Biru and I have an uproarious evening talking about the flip, drinking beer.

Sandeep Dwivedi

Sandeep Dwivedi, 39, is National Sports Editor, *The Indian Express*.

[After Pakistan's exit from the cricket World Cup in West Indies, news spread of their coach Bob Woolmer's death, just one of many curious stories Dwivedi was a witness to.]

A TELL-TALE NYLON NET AND THE CHANDERPAUL BACKWATERS

Award-winning Story

GEORGETOWN: As another crisp drive from twelve-year-old Brandon Chanderpaul spills out of the nylon net and rolls on the cemented front porch towards his grandfather Khemraj, a toothless smile dawns on the sun-beaten wrinkly face. The famous name that connects the two on the family tree isn't present at the in-house net session. You see him on television, fighting a losing battle against the New Zealanders in a World Cup game.

But Shivnarine's presence is always there at his family home with uneven architecture – the result of a gradual construction update, not a plinth-to-roof planned effort. A Man of the Match prize car squats uncomfortably in the congested porch that has three miniature shivlings on a corner platform.

Two hammocks hang nearby, almost encroaching on Brandon's play-zone. But one thing hasn't changed, from the mud house that Shiv grew up in, to the comfortable villa that Brandon is in today. It's the nylon net. It has only re-defined itself.

Khemraj and his forefathers used the net to fish. Today it spills out balls that Brandon hits as the Chanderpauls transformed themselves from modest fisher folk to an elite cricketing family with a former West Indian captain.

This happens to be one of the several success stories in the Unity Village, just an hour's bumpy drive down narrow dirt tracks from Georgetown.

For most living in the impressive wooden houses on stilts, dangerously close to the Atlantic Sea, tracing their roots means going back to 1834 when 414 indentured labourers landed in Guyana to work on sugarcane plantations.

Over the years, the Indo-Guyanese community has steadily climbed the social ladder. For example that boy, Bharrat Jagdeo, one is told, who used to live a stone's throw from the Chanderpaul house – and way inferior to Shiv as a cricketer – is the president of the country.

Our first destination in Unity Village is Beer Garden, also close to where Brandon is knocking the ball. The owner of the place – a pretty lady with Portuguese blood, Annalee – is Shiv's first wife, and mother of his only child. She talks about his estranged husband's early days of hardship before directing us to his in-laws' place.

The news has been relayed, and grandfather and grandson, bare-chested, are at the gate. Pleasantries exchanged, it is time to talk about the most likeable cricketer across the West Indies. (It's an eye-opener for any outsider that Brian Lara doesn't quite enjoy that status).

It's strange to notice that Khemraj's conversation revolves around Shiv only when he is talking in past tense. When it comes to the present, it's always about Brandon. The club cricketer with a deep knowledge of the game relishes talking about the days of grooming his son and the 'work in progress' grandson. Ask him if Shiv, who spends most of his time in Miami with his second wife, happens to drop in at Unity Village often and a monosyllabic 'sometimes' barely escapes from his mouth.

He soon switches to the early chapter of the story, one about a young boy with prodigious cricketing talent. He also loved to accompany his father to sea in his free time. But those were rare instances. Unity Village was more familiar with the sight of father and son moving towards a cricket field, not to a fishing trawler.

An abandoned building close by worked as indoor nets. 'I used to give him throw downs, but the concrete walls took a big toll on the balls. Those days the balls were not just expensive, but also tough to avail,' says Khemraj. The sight of a box full of balls of different colours and variety lying close to where Brandon is batting highlights the financial change that has come by.

Shiv's stance as the junior cricketer wasn't so prominently square on, according to Khemraj, but that was something he developed over the years.

Though Brandon's diagonally split legs when facing the underarm bowling in his courtyard makes the question 'who is he imitating' quite irrelevant.

'When he was very young, Shiv asked him to switch as a left-hander. And I saw to it that Brandon can throw with both his arms,' says Khemraj. Suddenly, one ends up gazing at the bony youngster, hoping to catch some deep insight into the rather ordinary looking expansive drive with the optimism of being one among the first few to spot the future ambidextrous prodigy so early.

It is tough to decide if it is the loving grandfather talking or a coach with a sharp eye when Khemraj says how Brandon just the other day scored a brilliant 60-plus score against a second division team and adds: 'He is better than what Shiv was at this age.'

If it's the coach talking, a trip down memory lane at Unity Village is a certainty for one when Brandon makes it big, besides, there will be a lot to look forward to for West Indies cricket.

Shiv's rise from a promising cricketer to an internationally proven star was the fastest. Khemraj switches to flashback. 'I used to take Shiv along to watch big cricket at Georgetown. I once saw that Indian leggie Chandrasekhar who was here for a club game,' he says.

In one club game, featuring West Indian captain Carl Hooper, the father asked his son to watch closely. 'I told him try to play like these players, they have international class,' he recalls.

It seems Shiv didn't bat an eyelid, soaked in everything he saw. In a few years he was rubbing shoulders with Hooper and shared a record-breaking stand with him in a Test match too.

By now Brandon has left the bat and is beside his grandfather. The boy hasn't spoken a word since this untimely intrusion. Very typical of his age, he stares at his feet whenever his name gets mentioned, but is wide-eyed when talk drifts to his father.

As one leaves and throws a final glance at the Chanderpaul home, the sight of two bare-chested, just in shorts, figures separated by a generation and nylon net in the background plays tricks with the mind. Temporarily they would pass off as fisher folk ready to start their day's work. That's when one realises that the nylon net is no longer used to catch fish but to spill out balls and the man who redesigned its more profitable use isn't there in the frame.

Personal Account

When the office asked me to pick a team, other than India, to follow during the 2007 World Cup in the Caribbean, I didn't quite lose sleep that night. For me ticking the Pakistan box on the complicated media accreditation form was a no-brainer. Me and Pakistan go back a long way. Except for a few days in the year when they played India, I was an unabashed fan of the temperamental men in green who wouldn't give an inch on their day but would meekly concede a mile the very next game.

With a cutout of Stefan Edberg playing ball on the glass door of my cupboard during teen days, it was apparent that consistency wasn't a virtue I rated too highly. For me a breathtaking backhand pass, a high-kicking top-spin serve, the graceful net approach for a killer volley mattered more than the juvenile Grand Slam count. Like the Swede tennis superstar of late '80s-early '90s, the Pakistan cricket team of that era had the originality and flair. Near scuffles and never-ending war of words with those who mixed geography with cricket made me grow closer to the not-so-popular neighbours.

Though, little did I know that my reflex choice to hang around my old favourite Pakistan would be seen as a calculated decision loaded with grave foresight in days to come. Pakistan didn't quite win the World Cup (that year the champion status of those very consistent out-of-this-world aliens in golden yellow was never in doubt) but they certainly proved to be the team to follow. This time around the unfortunate untimely death of their coach Bob Woolmer ensured that Pakistan lived up to its reputation of being in the news even when not doing well on field.

Being in Jamaica, Pakistan's base camp during the group games, proved to be the most challenging assignment since that watershed day of my life in mid-'90s when within days of getting my post-graduate physics degree I started getting paid to watch sports and write about it. During those heady days while seated in the best seat at stadiums with a laptop, never had I thought that covering cricket would one day take me to a hospital, mortuary, autopsy expert and police station. But that fortnight in Jamaica made me wiser about life. It made me think about the frailty of human life, the naivety of treating the modern sports as 'just a game' and the depressing realisation that the glorious uncertainties surrounding the game might just be dictated by some seedy syndicate.

It all started on a gloomy Sunday in March when coach Woolmer breathed his last in his hotel room a day after his team Pakistan was knocked out of the tournament following a shock loss to Ireland. At the start of the tournament when Pakistan was clubbed with West Indies, Zimbabwe, Ireland and with two of the four teams going to the next stage, it wasn't quite seen as the Group of Death. As it happens most times, death struck like a bolt from the blue.

Like many reporters covering that World Cup, I too have been often asked: Where were you when Woolmer died? Since the exact time of Woolmer's final walk to the pavilion is still debated, all I can say is I wasn't too far when his body was being discovered. I was in the hotel Pegasus lobby keeping a post-breakfast appointment fixed with the Pakistan coach the previous day. Suddenly, the missed exclusive Q&A about Pakistan's loss became irrelevant as there were other important questions to be asked and the man who knew those answers wasn't around. As fate would have it the reports that day weren't dissecting Pakistan's loss but the autopsy of their coach.

* * *

The tragedy overshadowed one of World Cup cricket's greatest feel-good story. A bunch of amateurs, who earned their living teaching school kids, delivering post and driving tankers; came to West Indies wearing Ireland shirts. A tie against Zimbabwe and the historic win over Pakistan gave their manager a healthy headache. He had to make calls to the employers of his humble World Cupper for extra leave since no one dreamt that they would reach the super league phase. Cinderella wasn't going home even after the midnight deadline.

On the sidelines of this Irish fairy tale I met a documentary maker Paul Davey, who with no grand future plans or budget outlays started filming the team since the time they qualified for World Cup. Even in his wildest dream he didn't expect that his docu drama would have such a climax. Davey was to become a friend as he too like me was at the right place at the right time. He struggled with finance to travel with his team on their unbelievable journey but somehow he managed to keep the camera rolling.

Days after the World Cup, Davey kept his promise and couriered a copy of the documentary that he later titled *Breaking Boundaries*. After it was telecast on BBC and Irish national television during Christmas, the documentary became a regular feature on the in-flight entertainment menu of several top airlines like British Airways, Sir Lankan Airways, Emirates and Aer Lingus. The last mail I got from Davey informed that Ireland's inspirational story was being screened at the Chicago film festival. And as if to compliment all this, Ireland was pushing hard at ICC to get Test status. In the March of 2007, while the world mourned the departure of a legendary coach, a cricketing nation was being born.

* * *

With the 2007 World Cup spread over several Caribbean countries, the discomfort of changing currency at every airport coincided with the pleasure of exploring new pastures after every landing. Guyana's Indian connection is all too famous to even mention and it proved to be a home away from home for me on that long trip. The first hint of that came on the first visit to the newly-constructed Providence cricket stadium.

As a popular number from the Salman Khan cult-hit *Tere Naam* blared from the public address system, I was greeted by a very familiar welcome by the office boy with a heavy Bengali accent at the Shapoorji Pallonji and Co. Limited – the Indian builders of the stadium site office. '*Chai piyenge*,' he says escorting one to his boss' makeshift chambers where sat an ever-smiling project manager, I Parthiban. 'Though India might have not reached Super Eight, the Providence stadium is an Indian success story,' he says introducing himself and his construction work.

As one takes leave Parthiban tries to fish out a business card but soon realises that he had passed on the last he had in his pocket to the Sri Lankan captain Mahela Jayawardene, who were here for the nets. The project manager would have loved it more in case it was Rahul Dravid there at the stadium. The Wall might have collapsed but the stadium stands tall.

To dig deep into the historical Indo-Guyanese bond, me and a few friends plan a trip to Unity Village – for the pure cricketing types Shivnarine Chanderpaul's birth place. It was here that shipload of North Indians landed in 1834 to work in sugarcane plantations. Generations later the settlers formed the backbone of West Indies cricket and one of them even went on to become the president of Guyana.

In the courtyard of one of the majestic stilted houses on the bank of the Atlantic Sea one met two less-famous Chanderpauls, separated by a generation. Shivnarine's son has a batting style very similar to his father's as in the presence of his grandfather he hits a few balls in the make-shift nets in the verandah. We take turns to bowl under arm at him and hope that some day we can claim that we saw the boy first.

Another memorable evening that week was running into a few famous cricketers at a famous Indian eating joint. Empty seats and tempting menu increased the hunger pangs. But we were soon stopped in our tracks. 'We have the Bangladesh World Cup cricketers here. Wait till they finish. In case there's something left, you get to eat,' said the lady owner, matter of factly.

After eyeing several rice plates disappear, aromatic daal reaching the nostrils but not a centimetre below it and gauging the taste of the thick brown mutton curry by numerous repeat orders came the ultimate anti-climax. An apologetic tone informed us that the wait was futile as the vessels in the kitchen were empty. That just meant another set of Indians were left high and dry by a bunch of hungry cricketers from Bangladesh.

From Guyana we move to Grenada, a tiny island nation that can be covered by car in a matter of hours. It turned out to be the place I wheel to meet a person who charges several hundred dollars for an hour's interaction. As a journalistic perk I get to spend several hours with one of the world's most celebrated sports psychologist, Rudi Webster, free. He famously tried to clear the mental cobwebs of Indian cricketers few months before the World Cup. Among the top sports professional who graced his couch is Tiger Woods. 'Yeah, right,' wasn't the kind of response that came to the back of my mind in 2007.

Sitting on the balcony of his luxurious house that squats majestically on a hill and overlooks a pristine white beach next to the clear azure sea that fails to hide the corals below, he asked several questions about life and answered a few queries too. After about an hour he asks, 'Ok, so what kind of an interview you want?' The trance is broken and I get the recorder out. As expected he didn't reveal much about his celebrated clients but still it was a rewarding interaction. The one Webster line that stayed with me till date was his observation about the Indian cricket team that was down in dumps at that time. 'The soil is very fertile. People are very hard on them but they have the potential,' he said. Before the next World Cup, India went on to be World No.1 team.

* * *

Barbados was the final destination and the culmination of a crazy ride. Asian hearts continued to break in West Indies that year as Sri Lanka were outplayed in the final by the Aussies. Adam Gilchrist with a squash ball in his glove smashes everything in sight and the Islanders failed to conquer the world. Early morning a day after the final I ventured to the ground and saw a few beer bottles littered around the pitch. Being a Sunday the cleaners haven't yet arrived. The tell-tale signs of Aussie celebration at Kensington Oval were still in place. Close to the temporary stage, where the Aussies marched to collect their third straight World Cup trophy, tiny shinning ticker tape glowed brightly in the hard morning sun. The party was over and it was time to leave for home.

Totally exhausted, I re-schedule my ticket to take the first flight home. Yes, even the sights in Caribbean can bore you. Waiting at the airport reading a borrowed cricket book I once again realise how my reflex choice would be perceived as a calculated decision loaded with grave foresight by some. The sight of Aussies in their formals with silverware in most luggage trolleys told me that as luck would have it the world champions too had transit flight to catch from Heathrow. Before I left home friends ribbed me about the jinx I carry with me. They have statistics on their fingertips, which prove that my presence in the press box translates into Zaheer Khan bowling too many wides and Sachin Tendulkar edging away moving balls to the keeper. I scoffed at them saying that this time I will bring the World Cup home. I kept my word: the famous silverware was on board when I took off from Barbados. Now, I can't be blamed if the Indians flew out early.

Savita Vikram Harkare

Savita Vikram Harkare, 43, is
Chief Sub-editor, *Lokmat*,
Nagpur.

[A majority of women found out that they were HIV Positive when they became pregnant. Many had been infected by their husbands who had not revealed their status at the time of their marriage.]

CUD CHEWING IN THE REALMS OF REALITY

Personal Account

Like the ever-neglected patients of HIV/AIDS, the topic of HIV/AIDS has also remained a taboo for the hoi polloi.

When I met a doctor on 1 December – the AIDS Eradication Day – in search of important statistics – I stumbled upon the stark fact that AIDS transcends all fashionable terms used in statistical jugglery. It spoofs at the society as a much bigger problem.

Shashi contracted HIV infection at the young age of twenty-six. However, more than this, her valiant battle against the social stigma on one hand and the terminal illness on the other, had left her mentally battered.

When she was first diagnosed with the infection, doctors even refused to touch her. She immediately sensed that something terrible had happened to her. Her husband who came to visit her two days later, however, offered her a strange gift: a set of divorce papers.

Since then the word 'society' has become anathema for her.

However, Shashi is not alone battling the disease and the stigma attached to it. There are many of her ilk – who are ploughing a lonely furrow.

Swati's child was born fifteen days after her husband died of AIDS. An employee of GMCH, Swati tried to pull her feet into prostitution after she was cast off by the society. Desperate at her situation, she observed quite lugubriously, 'Though we are ostracised by the society, the same society wants to enjoy carnal pleasure from us.'

In a shocking incident at Merath Medical College in Uttar Pradesh, the doctors refused to deliver the baby of a woman who had undergone labour pains because she was HIV positive. At last, her husband was forced to deliver the baby.

This was the first ever incident in the history of India. However, after the death of her husband she was thrown out of her house by her in-laws.

My detailed study into the social malaise further revealed the dark side of the story. At all levels, only women are the ultimate sufferers. Though the central government, USAIDS and Bill Clinton Foundation are willing to spend crores of rupees, the moot question is how beneficial are these efforts for the uplift of women.

Today, judicial battles for the rights of children born of HIV-infected parents have become a norm. Though more debates are taking place nowadays at national and international fora regarding human rights of HIV-hit population, there is no gainsaying the fact that this segment of the society is ostracised and their human rights are trampled upon. This is despite the fact that fifteen HIV-infected women in a press conference held in Chennai, unmasked their faces and courageously told the world, 'Yes we have got a right to lead life on our own terms'.

In another incident, a married woman announced before a strong gathering in Nagpur that she was HIV positive. All these incidents are a pointer towards the struggle of these women to wriggle out of their just predicament.

HIV/AIDS is not only a health-related problem, but also a social, familial, pshychological, economic and legal handicap staring into the face of the world. The problem becomes more complex in case of women. In India, out of a two crore HIV-infected population, nearly 50 per cent comprises of women.

All these women are leading a sub-human life in the absence of family support, and in the face of financial weakness, social boycott and negligent healthcare for themselves and their kids. The problem gets compounded if their husband and the children in the family are also HIV positive.

There are problems and questions, however, these women can not discuss them openly. Hence they are faced with an embarrassing situation as to whom they should ask their questions and wherefrom to source the needed information. The only exception is the women associated with Positive Network.

As per the data provided by research institutes, it is feared that only 50 per cent of the HIV-infected patients come out in the open and take treatment. There are almost an equal number of people suffering from hidden HIV infections.

Anathema and misunderstanding are both said to be responsible for this sorry state of affairs.

Hence, time has come to honestly review our responsibility and role as a society.

Though the government and social service organisations have been spending crores of rupees on HIV/AIDS control, the government has miserably failed to create awareness about this malady and provide proper medical care. The expenditure of ART Firstline is Rs 1100-3500 per month. This expenditure reaches upto Rs 10,000 per month in ART Second line. Though free medicines are distributed in government-run ART centres, many patients are left deprived of this benefit. On many occasions, they are not even aware of the facility.

Poignantly, 86.5 per cent women among rural tribes of Vidarbha have not even heard of this malaise – and they do not know what HIV/AIDS is all about.

This grim picture came to light during a recent survey conducted by *Lokmat* in the six districts of Vidarbha. In the survey, women were nudged to talk about HIV/AIDS. Gadchiroli, Amravati, Yavatmal, Chandrapur, Bhandara and Wardha districts were the six districts selected for this survey.

Under the survey, 110 women from tribal and rural areas were asked about HIV/AIDS. Of them, 95 women admitted that they did not know what HIV/AIDS was. Only 15 women (13.5 per cent) knew of this deadly disease, while 9 women had only heard it mentioned on radio.

All these women are totally ignorant of HIV/AIDS; and also of the mode of infection and the preventive measures that should be adopted to thwart its infection.

The survey has brought to the fore a startling fact that the government health machinery – which is juggling with statistics and a slew of civil service organisations which are receiving lakhs of rupees from foreign agencies – have never stepped into these areas.

During the survey, women were also asked whether social service organisations, primary health centres and other government hospitals forked out information about this disease and whether awareness campaigns were organised in their areas.

Of the 110 women, 101 informed that no information is dished out in government hospitals while only 9 women said that information was given to them. However, all of them claimed that no social service organisation working on HIV/AIDS operated in their areas.

The government has made HIV test mandatory for pregnant women. However, only a handful were aware of this development. 106 women quizzed by *Lokmat* were completely in dark about pregnant women being required to undergo this test or that HIV test was done in hospitals. Despite the number of HIV/AIDS patients on the rise in all these districts during the last five years, public awareness about this disease is dismal.

According to official statistics, the number of HIV/AIDS affected people has crossed 10,000. However, in reality, this figure is much higher. In Nagpur district alone, 25,000 people are affected by HIV/AIDS.

AIDS patients have been detected in the remotest Mallampodur hamlet in Bhamragarh tehsil of Gadchiroli. Similarly, the number of HIV/AIDS infected patients is rapidly rising at Chikhaldara and Dharni tehsils of Melghat. Last year, AIDS claimed ten lives. Large scale exploitation of women, growing trend of migration, prevalence of quacks and absence of general awareness have caused this hydra-headed monster to spread its tentacles inside the rural belt of Vidarbha. However, no concrete steps to control this menace is in sight.

Several hundred youths from Vidarbha who have contracted HIV/AIDS are being pushed to the jaws of death following proliferation of bogus doctors in the region due to the expanding waiting list at ART centres of the government and the false promises of these bogus doctors to treat HIV positive patients.

As per the statistics of the Maharashtra State AIDS Control Committee, ART centres are located at five places in Vidarbha which are Government Medical College and Hospital, Nagpur, Akola, Yavatmal, Chandrapur and Wardha. However, only centres at Nagpur, Yavatmal and Akola are functional currently. Extreme shortage of medicines is another shortcoming. The condition of Integrated Coordination and Treatment Centres (ICTC) is also not very good. There are 604 ICTCs in the state. Many of these centres do not have the kits required for the diagnosis of HIV infection. As a result, many blood samples remain untested. Patients from inaccessible villages of Bhamragad tehsil in Gadchiroli district are forced to visit Chandrapur for ART and CD4 tests, which is a burden for these poor patients. As a result, many patients die without proper treatment. Many NGOs who have gobbled up funds have vanished giving the quacks an opportune time to feather their own nests.

The pastors, hakims, vaids, priests, allopathic, ayurvedic and homoeopathy doctors are minting money by taking advantage of the situation.

These fake doctors claim that they can cure AIDS/HIV infection within a month, forcing the patients to take recourse to them and finally get duped. A large number of such cases have been exposed. Sanjay (name changed) fell victim to one of the quacks. He allegedly disposed of his field and house for treatment.

However, he did not become negative from positive. The treatment also damaged one of his eyes. As on date, he is being provided second line treatment.

Another patient Joseph (name changed) was undergoing anti-retroviral therapy. A pastor advocated him a mantra for salvation from HIV infection. Joseph discontinued the treatment and chanted the mantras. Some days later he died.

According to an NGO working with HIV/AIDS affected people around 400-500 people have lost their lives by reposing faith in such bogus doctors. The high percentage of flitting population is said to be responsible for the spread of HIV/AIDS virus.

Many other cases have come to light where the breadwinners of the family, having stayed out for 5-6 months, had returned home with HIV infection. The percentage of migrants is more in border areas of the state.

In urban areas, the percentage of daily wagers coming from inaccessible rural parts is increasing. In Nagpur city alone, currently more than one lakh migratory labourers are working. Their percentage is likely to go up in the coming years. These labourers stay in Nagpur for 4-5 months. The unsafe sex practised during this period and exploitation of female labourers, has pushed this strata of the society into the clutches of this malaise.

Similarly, a large number of population also settles down in the district for bamboo cutting. The transporters also bring hordes of people who are employed by the forest department for its extensive work. Nagpur city and the surroundings have approximately 250 brick kilns. In these brick kilns, which are located at Bina, Ranala, Kauta, Thasal, Masali Birgaon, Vinoba Bhave Nagar, Alam Nagar, Parseoni Road, Khaparkheda, six thousand migrant labourers work.

These labourers usually come from Uttar Pradesh, Bihar, and Madhya Pradesh. Bharatiya Adim Jati Sewak Sangh, in association with AVERT is creating awareness among these brick kiln labourers about HIV/AIDS.

Indian Institute of Youth Welfare is running a campaign in Subhash Nagar, Goa Colony, Raj Nagar, Kachi Pura, Indira Nagar, Cotton Market, Dashrath Nagar, Sudam Puri and Ekatamata Nagar localities, where the majority of population is of migrant labour.

In 2004-05, sixteen males and seven females; in 2005-06, five males and ten females; and in 2006-07, ten males, nine females and four kids were found to have contracted HIV infection. A large segment of the migrant population is still ignorant of HIV/ AIDS threat.

When NACO and AVERT have included the migrant population under dangerous category, it is important to run a project for migrant population not only in Nagpur but also in other parts of Vidarbha.

In Vidarbha, there are 1136 rural hospitals in 11 districts. It is a need of the hour to start ART facility in all these hospitals and Integrated Co-ordination and Treatment Centre at Primary Health Centres.

I scouted the remotest part of Vidarbha on behalf of *Lokmat* and interacted with hundreds of women. To my shocking discovery, I found that nearly 86 per cent women do not know what AIDS is all about.

For AIDS control, people's awareness is the only control. I have prided in recollecting the contribution of *Lokmat* in this direction. I am also waiting for the day when the entire society would change its attitude towards HIV/AIDS and view the malady positively. That day would be most satisfying for me – and as significant a milestone as this highest award of the land in the field of printed journalism!

Avert Society was founded in November 2001 under National AIDS Control Programme by Maharashtra State AIDS Control Committee (MSACC), Mumbai District AIDS Control Committee (MDACC) and National AIDS Control Society (NACS).

The government has made highest financial allocation to combat this malady of all other diseases in the country. Apart from this, US AIDS, World Health Organisation, Bill Clinton Foundation and Bill Gates are pumping crores of rupees for battling this disease.

In 2008-09 budget, Rs 16,534 crore were earmarked for health sector, of which Rs 993 crore have been allocated for National AIDS Control programme. Last year Rs 969 crore were earmarked for this programme. The main thrust of the programme was to prevent HIV transmission from mother to the child. However, as a large chunk of population is deprived of this campaign, control of AIDS has become impossible and statistics are illusory.

The mode of combating this deadly infection is faulty in so much as a targeted area is selected for controlling the infection and all efforts are concentrated in that area – to the exclusion of other areas where it is found to be spreading rapidly. As a result, the number of patients, contrary to expectations, is going up. Active participation of the population is essential to prevent its spread. Only then this hydra-headed monster can be kept under check.

Sayli Udas Mankikar

Sayli Udas Mankikar, 31, is Special Correspondent with the *Hindustan Times*.

[Sayli Udas questions the policy of the gymkhanas in Mumbai which were not open to the public. She discovers the political nexus behind the unfair government policy.]

RESIDENTS WIN OVER KHAR GYMKHANA

Award-winning Story

Hindustan Times reporting put the grab of open spaces on the public agenda. The pressure grew when 16 of Mumbai's most prominent people on November 26 sent *Hindustan Times* an open letter demanding the policy be scrapped. Meanwhile, citizens continue their battle

Round 1: Residents win over Khar gymkhana.

For once, it was the members of an elite club built on public land, who were left out in the cold.

The office of Tony Khar Gymkhana was sealed, leaving members with no choice but to return home from the gates. Off limits to local residents for 75 years, ever since the ground was leased out for safe keeping, it also often hosted weddings and functions, causing traffic snarls and noise pollution.

According to lease regulations there should be no commercial activities on the ground and citizens should be allowed entry to recreation grounds. Gymkhana president Sundar Sadnani declined comment. 'We will abide by the rules,' he said.

Over two years, the residents wrote scores of letter to the Collector's office and repeatedly met with officials to try and regain accesses to their public ground with no success.

As the civic body considered handing out 49 more open spaces for adoption, the residents began to press harder for action. Finally, the Collector responded dispatching a team headed by Tehsildar Manisha Gavande to seal the office.

On 13 November, a resident meet was organised with the Collector to plead for action against the club. A resident said, on condition of anonymity, 'Finally we got a response.'

Suburban Collector Vishwas Patil admitted there were 'continuous representations' from residents on the issue. 'We decided to seal the office so that they abided by the rules,' he said.

The office was sealed for three hours. According to Patil, the Gymkhana management has now promised in writing to abide by the lease agreement.

The Khar Gymkhana has over 7000 members and the club building occupies more than 25 per cent of the plot. 'The membership fee is around Rs 15 lakh, how can we join?' asked Anandini Thakoor of the Khar Residents' Association.

The Violations

1. No commercial activities are allowed on the grounds, but the club held weddings and private parties.

2. Loudspeakers regularly crossed the 10 p.m. deadline set by the Supreme Court, said residents. Moreover, members often flouted the parking rules and parked vehicles wherever they wanted, locals said.

3. None of the club's facilities were open to non-members and with a Rs 15-lakh entry fee, most local residents could not afford to join.

Too Little, Too Late, Says Collector

Confirms Khar Gym hosted weddings without sanction, promises action

Five days after *Hindustan Times* reported how Mumbai Suburban collector Vishwas Patil sealed the Khar Gymkhana for flouting guidelines, the trustees submitted the club's records to him as promised.

Hours after he received the reports, Patil confirmed that the club has in the past few days hosted weddings without his permission, flouting rules.

The Gymkhana, which is the property of the Mumbai Suburban collectorate, has also not allowed entry to non-members, besides creating problems of traffic and pollution in the surrounding area, residents allege. From 2005, the Khar Residents' Association has been complaining against the club, following which the collector took action.

'The club hosted weddings at the open tennis courts every

single day without permission. They have flouted the rules, but we have done panchanamas on each day,' said Patil, who says he was waiting for the club to submit its records first. 'Now appropriate action will be taken.'

'We have written to both the collector and the auditor general to appropriately check records and to take action on the club for flouting rules,' said Anandini Thakoor, association chairperson.

Fight Club

- Mumbai Suburban Collector Viswas Patil sealed the offices of Khar Gymkhana, for not following rules, on 29 November.
- The Gymkhana, however, kept its grounds closed to the public.

Personal Account

Winning the first Prakash Kardaley award for civic journalism was a great honour and a dream come true for me. First, because it is in the name of a great editor, the former resident editor of *The Indian Express*, Pune, who was well known for his work in bringing in the Right To Information Act (RTI), a tool for transparency.

More importantly, it is an award that gave recognition to a beat which, because it deals with city drains, potholes, garbage management, is not considered as glamorous as beats like defence, civil aviation, government, etc.

What I found fascinating about civic journalism is that any issue that you write about is directly related to the citizen who pays taxes to the corporation to run the city. As a reporter you become an agent of communication between these important wings in the city and the public.

I started to cover the civic beat in the heavy rains of Mumbai in the August of 2005. I still remember the day when I entered the grand art deco building of the Brihanmumbai Municipal Corporation, half-drenched. I was looking for information on rainfall and I was guided to a ground floor disaster management room.

The officer looked at me, asked me to sit. I asked him for information on rainfall: how much rain, where, any incidents, felled trees, the usual. He said that I looked new to the beat. I replied in the affirmative. I asked him how he knew. He said reporters do not come to the civic corporation before 2 p.m. and I was there at 11 a.m. Second, he said people first have a cup of hot tea and then talk business.

These were two of the unwritten rules of covering the civic beat which I learnt on day one but never forgot. I set my own rules: I still set foot in the corporation office by noon.

I love the building and its grandeur and of course the canteen that served subsidised *vada-pav*, my staple diet. While I covered several issues during my four-year stint as a civic reporter, one of the most successful was taking on the civic corporation, the collector's office and the revenue department of the Mumbai government on the issue of open spaces and gymkhanas in the city.

The issue of open spaces first came up during my stint at *The Indian Express* in early 2007 when a proposal tabled at the Improvements Committee of the civic corporation proposed that spaces above 15,000 square metre would be given to private parties for building clubs. The idea was to be able to provide sporting amenities to the public.

But past experience of such spaces given to private builders had left a bad taste in the city of Mumbai. A similar proposal tabled in 2002 saw 10 such spaces given to politicians. All of them had built luxurious clubs on public grounds, charged astronomical fees and denied access to non-members. It was not difficult to imagine what would happen if over 40 such spaces, the size of 4 football grounds each, were given away – it would leave no large, wide open spaces in the city. Apart from depriving children of playing areas, it also reduced the absorption capacity of the ground for rainwater, one of the main reasons that Mumbai is seeing an increased amount of water logging every passing year.

All the reporters covering the issue for the newspapers took it up, while a city organisation, Citispace, working on the issue of urban spaces supported us through facts. It provided us with information on the spaces that the city would lose. I highlighted the plight of the spaces given earlier and grilled the additional municipal commissioner on the issue. The pressure created by the press coverage forced the committee to not take up the proposal.

In November 2007, when I joined *Hindustan Times,* the issue had resurfaced. The day I joined *Hindustan Times*, my colleague who covered the civic body prior to me had run a series on the issue. It brought back the issue to the forefront. After the opening story, the baton was passed on to me.

I realised that this issue had been written about over and over again but was not creating the kind of pressure required to put a stop to the policy altogether. Keeping it on the backburner was dangerous. I sat with Citispace and we jointly charted out a plan to highlight this issue every single day to create public opinion.

I wrote on the amount spent on buying cars from our tax money by the mayor and the politicians holding key posts in the corporation was enough to protect and maintain the spaces they were ready to sell off. I spoke to an international expert on the dangers of giving away open spaces and the flood risk it could create. *Hindustan Times* bombarded the city with such stories every day for a fortnight.

On the day the proposal came up in the improvements committee again, citizens lined up to protest outside the hall. Nothing happened, the proposal was passed.

Then, we went all out. Citizens wrote an open letter to the chief minister signed by eminent citizens which *Hindustan Times* published. While another group of citizens started their protest against the Khar Gymkhana located in Mumbai's western suburbs. The Gymkhana had started using its public space for giving out for weddings, creating noise and denying any public access to its grounds. The lease had also lapsed. Twenty such gymkhanas, mainly in south Mumbai and the suburbs belonged to the British era and had been given on 39 to 99-year leases by the concerned collector. The agreement specified that a part of the leased land had to be accessible to public. Almost none were.

We highlighted the plight of non-members and how they had been denied access to these gymkhanas. A 100-year-old policy had to change. Citizens took to the streets. Khar residents along with Citispace had public meetings, street plays, the pressure was built up every single day. With citizens, I met Chief Minister Vilasrao Deshmukh, followed by a meeting with Revenue Minister Narayan Rane. At *Hindustan Times*, we kept up our campaign.

Following the protests, Narayan Rane decided to amend the gymkhana policy. The Khar Gymkhana was asked to put a stop to any commercial activity, the weddings were banned. A new policy is now in place that ensures the Gymkhana keeps some space accessible to public at all hours at no cost. Failing this, the lease will be cancelled. The chief minister also ordered a stay on the civic policy on open spaces following heated opposition in the state assembly.

Both these decisions were a victory of sorts for civic reportage with citizen involvement. What next?

Even after I received the Kardaley Award in April 2009, I felt my job as a reporter remains incomplete. I have graduated to covering the Maharashtra government beat. I still fear, however, that one day the policy regarding open spaces will be changed and they will gradually disappear.

I always thought that discussing or highlighting a problem is easy but finding a solution is difficult, and something we hardly do. Therefore, I decided to pursue the issue further and seek a solution. I tried to find out how other civic bodies were handling their open spaces, and I got several inputs. One was feasible: develop spaces on the Delhi Development Authority (DDA) model where they develop sporting facilities through a tendering process while keeping the management to themselves and charged reasonable fees.

Hindustan Times editors jumped at the idea. A colleague in Delhi and I charted a two-page package on how Delhi did it, the costs involved and if it is was possible for Mumbai to implement the same model.

The story received a great response. A state minister actually travelled to Delhi to see what we had written about and the urban development department said it was a plan worth considering.

I have made a promise to myself: I will see to it that Mumbai's open spaces are saved from land sharks for a better and greener tomorrow. It would be unfair not to mention that this commitment to the issue would not be possible without the backing of the newspaper I am working for and the citizens who took up the issue.

Shital Morjaria

Shital Morjaria, 36, is
Programming Head with TV9.

[In hamlets close to Hyderabad, largescale hysterectomies were performed on unsuspecting women.]

FAILED HEALTH SYSTEMS AND UNWARRANTED HYSTERECTOMIES

Personal Account

In my three years experience of producing *Naveena*, the daily show on women and society for the Telugu Channel TV9, I have come across several heart-warming stories about women and their achievements that I have showcased through the series. There were many distressing aspects about women's lives that I covered on a regular basis through *Naveena* and the report that went on to win the Ramnath Goenka Excellence in Journalism Award shook up many people. It came as a chilling reminder of the newer forms of exploitation that some vulnerable sections of women, in particular, were facing. The report was about large-scale hysterectomies being performed in a few hamlets close to Hyderabad. The exposure of the case is closely related to the journey of the show itself. In many ways the effective coverage of the award-winning case would not have been possible without the path *Naveena* had staked out earlier.

The Winning Story

When I first heard the news I could not decide which of the two problems was worse: Menopause at twenty-five years or hysterectomies for ailments as routine as abdominal pain? Both these disturbing dimensions were essential parts of what was taking place in Kowdipally Mandal of Medak district in Andhra Pradesh. From among the 125 families who lived in the mandal, hysterectomy cases were reported from every second household. More than 700 women from two villages were operated upon for removal of the uterus, accompanied at times by the removal of the ovaries as well. Even girls as young as nineteen had undergone hysterectomies. Almost all the women who were operated upon were poor and uneducated lambada (tribal) women. The irony was that the women had to give up their land and life savings for a procedure that cost them their uterus as well as anything between Rs 15,000-Rs 50,000.

The *Naveena* team first came across some of these shocking facts through a newspaper article that carried the findings of a survey conducted by CARPED (Center for Action Research and People's Development), an organisation working in the mandal. We decided to carry out our own investigations. *Naveena* spoke at length to women from Kannaram and Mohammad Nagar villages in Kowdipally Mandal, visited the Primary Health Care Centres (PHCC) in the village, paid a surprise visit to the ayurveda doctor who had conducted most of the hysterectomies and checked the medical records of all the women who had undergone operations.

Most of these unfortunate women had approached the doctor with gynecological problems such as white discharge, pain in the stomach, cysts or urinary infections. In each case, the ayurveda doctor told them that the problem was very serious, that it could get worse and that they could even die if the uterus was not removed very quickly. As a consequence, his practice thrived while the women's health degenerated either with increased pain, menopause or subsequent illnesses for which they had to again seek medical help. As one of the women who had undergone the operation told us, 'My back aches terribly, I cannot bend. Earlier even with the pain I felt a lot better. Now it has become worse.'

Our findings from the investigation were depressing:

- The majority of the women were in the age group of 19-40. Many of them were unmarried.
- Some of them had been deserted by their husbands since they could not work or have children.
- Most women had sideffects in terms of severe pains or other health problems.
- The women were poor and became victims of the huge loans they took at exorbitant rates of interest in order to pay for the surgeries.

- The women complained that the government Primary Health Care (PHC) Centre did not cater to their medical problems because it was hardly ever open.

After our investigation, the *Naveena* team broke the story on television. The impact of the telecast was heartening. We were told that the doctor had closed down his practice and disappeared, the PHC cleaned up its act to the extent of keeping the clinic open and providing a gynaecologist once a month. The women had become more aware of their health needs and shared information among themselves about their experiences with the health system. Gynaecologists from Hyderabad who conducted medical camps in the mandal for the tribal women admitted that they had their own suspicions about the hysterectomy racket but had not been able to prevent them. They were appreciative of our programme that had provided them a context to raise the issue more forcefully with the women and the health department.

The Making of *Naveena:* The Unmaking of a Women's Show

When we started *Naveena*, a daily women's show in 2006, we were flooded with suggestions from various quarters for makeovers and for introducing cooking and diet concepts. As we struggled to put across our vision and wriggled out of acting upon the suggestions being offered, people thought us strange and difficult: through our show we had chosen career over cosmetics, women's news over fashion and ordinary inspirational stories over sensational coverage. Of course, it took a little while to effectively package the show but we did succeed against all odds and *Naveena* evolved into a daily programme in the afternoon band focused on empowering women with information on their rights and questioning discriminatory norms against them. What motivated us to develop this kind of show was our disappointment and anger with the stereotypical portrayal of women in films, television serials, and news coverage in the mainstream media as a whole. Women in serials were being portrayed either as victims and wrongdoers or as home-makers and home-breakers! In films they were sex objects conscious about their looks, but also vulnerable, sentimental and easily given to tears. There was a clear gap between women's everyday lives and the exaggerated representations of them.

Regional television in Andhra Pradesh had already defined women's show as a 'homemakers' show. The shows were, and still are, about makeup, lifestyle products, and about how to be perfect housewives. Some of the chat shows also focused on women's traditional domestic roles or portrayed them as achievers. Then there were the weekly chat shows on topical issues. Through their treatment of the subject matter, the broadcast media seemed to reconfirm traditional gender roles and promoted unrealistic ideals of chastity, passivity and the dependency of women in a way that reinforced a patriarchal outlook.

The 'everydayness' of women's emotions and aspirations as they went through their personal and professional lives were missing from these programmes. This is where *Naveena* stepped in to fill the critical gap. For example, *Naveena* focused on gynaecological problems that many women face as a routine but do not seek help. When it came to economic independence, we conveyed information about how to execute simple tasks like opening a bank account, getting a driver's license or a PAN card. We aired episodes on the legal rights of women whether it was maintenance, property rights or the effective procedures through which domestic violence could be tackled. *Naveena* took up various campaigns like 'Eve Teasing', 'Dark is Beautiful', 'NRI fraud marriages', 'Unknown Faces in Sports', and 'Marital Rape'.

While the first year was dedicated to the campaign mode, in the second year we moved to a magazine format where we introduced the viewers to news relevant to women's daily lives, their careers; we discussed nutrition for girls and women, and also included a segment on cooking that addressed the men. In the third year we introduced a more interactive mode where women (either by being present in the studio or through phone-ins) shared problems in their personal or professional lives and through *Naveena* we tried finding solutions to them. We also brought in experts to directly talk to our viewers about breast cancer, career counselling, and mental health. Apart from these segments, we incorporated investigative stories on women prisoners, *joginis* and *hijras* and also on issues such as security concerns women face in public places during the night.

Naveena managed to distinguish itself from other women's shows not only in terms of its content but also through its packaging. Where most women's shows opted for a softer look through their use of pastel shades, *Naveena*'s look was bold, making no concession to received wisdom about what women's show should comprise. The background musical score was strong, made even more so through the use of hard-hitting soundbites. The graphics for the show provided telling statistics on the subject that was being discussed and the anchor of the programme was portrayed as a strong and modern woman. The idea was to create a new image of the contemporary woman who was self-sufficient, confident and bold about voicing her opinions.

We also included toll free numbers of different helplines on our show. When women approached us for help we directed them to our regular panel of guests who were lawyers, activists, feminists, counsellors and doctors. I am proud that *Naveena* took up issues that no other programme had ever done, whether at the regional or national level. For instance, we did a series on breasts: right from the correct bra size to campaigns on breast cancer. On air, we talked about marital rape. We did episodes on problems women have if their partners suffer from premature ejaculation. And in a lighter vein we also had a cookery show for men, which was called 'Superman!'. The range of issues we tackled and the impact we had would not have been possible without the contributions of every member of the team – right from the anchor and the coordinator to the cameraperson and the editor and the graphics in-charge. All the people associated with the making of *Naveena* owned up the programme completely and worked as a team right through.

In January 2006, *Naveena* introduced its own contest – the Naveena Mahila Contest. Fed up with beauty contests, we decided to honour women from the grassroots who had shown extraordinary courage. The Mahila Contest was an effort to showcase the struggles of these women and to also share their inspiring stories with public. The awards were instituted for three categories: (i) fighting for one's right; (ii) fighting against a social evil; and (iii) showing courage in any situation of their life. Beginning with 2006, the contest has honoured women each year on International Women's Day (8 March).

In the context of mainstream television where stereotyping women and sensational journalism sans ethics easily take over, I strongly believe that a programme like *Naveena* is important.

While I accept the criticism on behalf of my news channel for being a part of the 'breaking news' phenomenon, there is no other channel that could have sustained *Naveena* every day for three years. It occurs to me that a show such as *Naveena* was only to have been expected from a channel like TV9 that has the tagline 'For a Better Society' as its motto. In fact, this tagline was my inspiration when I joined TV9 as a reporter. It continues to motivate my work with the organisation.

Looking back on the journey so far, I realise that when one breaks norms, does something bold, unmakes or redefines something, there are many hurdles. For instance, we were branded 'feminists' when we talked about domestic violence, as 'men haters' when we spoke about marital rape and 'lesbians' when we spoke of same sex love. We, however, continued to highlight topics that mainstream society would find uncomfortable but that would eventually help vulnerable women navigate their lives better.

Winning the Ramnath Goenka Award (and also the UNFP Laadli Award previously in 2008) was hugely encouraging because the fight can get lonely at times. When the same work is recognised by two different awards, its worth is reconfirmed. Such recognition is especially important for us within the broadcast media because of the immense pressure exerted by the system of TRPs. Unfortunately, we in the mainstream media have not developed a method of measuring the impact of a show focused on social change in ways that can counter the pressure of TRPs. *Naveena* is a show about our lives, our struggles and our aspirations as women. Though social change in a patriarchal society is slow it is sure to happen. I believe that this fight of ours for social change will succeed as it takes place in diverse spheres. The mainstream medium of television is one such critical domain and my location here enables me to contribute to the many efforts that seek to redefine the world. The particular story about the unwarranted hysterectomies on tribal women as well as the many other stories we covered through *Naveena* are in equal measure a part of this ongoing effort.

Shoma Chaudhury

Shoma Chaudhury is
Managing Editor with weekly
newsmagazine, *Tehelka*.

[Shoma Chaudhury talks about subjects ranging from journalism to politics, from Islam to media-saturated figures, Shah Rukh Khan and Aamir Khan, and manages to bring freshness to her interviews.]

THE CONJUROR OF IMPROBABLE DREAMS

Award-winning Story

We are a ragtag group in a small, bare room. No more than six or seven. On the wall before us, a little boy with impossible teeth is darting with an infectious comet-like energy through his little life. Neighbourhood fights, exasperated parents, scowling teachers, undone homework. He's always in trouble, but there is something brilliantly joyous about him. You can't help smiling in the dark. Then the darkness starts to deepen. The little comet can't preserve its light. The little boy droops before our eyes.

And then, a flute note.

Superstar Aamir Khan's directorial debut, *Taare Zameen Par* (TZP) cannot get further from what one would expect. It has none of the staples of Bollywood: no fancy camerawork, no glitzy song, no triple star cast. None of the vanities of a first film from a man who could have all of it at a whim. TZP is just a simple story, simply told. Its effect is evident now in the small, bare room. Like the rest of us, Arshad, twenty-three, is in tears. 'I know that helpless feeling. It took me back to when I was in Class III,' says he. 'I was so bad at maths I slipped a suicide note under my parents' pillow. I was crying thinking of what the world expects of all of us.'

That is the secret of Aamir's magical film. It speaks to everyone. On the face of it, TZP might be about a dyslexic boy crushed until an empathetic art teacher rescues him, but at its core, it's about the world's imprisoning expectations. Quick-eyed Ishaan Awasthi, mesmerised by puddles and tadpoles, is the face – the aching remembrance – of the free spirit each of us had as a child before we were benchpressed into adulthood.

'The film puts you in touch with all the small emotions we've lost in our over-hurried lives.' Cinematographer Baba Azmi calls it 'one of the most important films in our country now.'

Important, because like *Rang De Basanti*, TZP is certain to trigger crucial new conversations. RDB divined the sleeping idealism beneath India's cynical urban youth. TZP touches a deeper and forbidden subject: the intensely personal world of children, parents and differing abilities. Reshma Jiwani, mother of a twenty-seven-year-old son with learning difficulties, talks of the immensely difficult journey they had to make as a family. 'My daughter was excellent at studies, but my son couldn't cope. Both went to Bombay Scottish. When my son was twelve, he sank into depression. We couldn't understand what was happening. There were no facilities. We sent him away to a military school in Pune. There was so much hurt and antagonism. Then he met a teacher, Medha. She helped him hugely. He was a six-footer in Class VII and played great basketball. She put him in touch with his own special skills. The turning point came when I learnt to accept he was different.'

TZP almost exactly mirrors Reshma Jiwani's story. And a million others. In the overheated world of new age parenting, counsellors and teachers across the country are struggling to shift the paradigm. 'Parents don't know how to leave kids be. They are so conformist, so competitive, they even compete about children's hobbies and where they should go in their free time,' says Carole Paul, a special educator with The Step by Step World School in Delhi.

'Parents forget children are like stem cells,' says Annie Koshy, principal, St Mary's, Delhi. 'They can take any shape, become anything. You can't squeeze them into the figure you want. Education should be a romance, an adventure, a mystery, an opportunity to find the secret gift of every child. Not a regimentation.'

Because Aamir is a superstar in the most powerful cultural medium of our time, because his films are always rooted in the language of mass entertainment, and because Ishaan Awasthi is played to haunting perfection by saucy little Darsheel Safary, 8, discovered in a Shiamak Dawar class, TZP is bound to slip into people's bloodstream and effect subconscious emotional transformations. A flute note in the noise. A reminder of the healing power of acceptance, imagination and play – the 'fresh birth of everything', as Tejal Chheda, mother of one of the child actors, puts it.

Aamir himself has always had a gift for hearing this flute note in the noise. In following that note, in trusting its lone and often difficult call, he's radically altered the industry. 'Only Aamir could've made TZP,' says Rakeysh Mehra. 'Ten years ago, every star was doing several films at the same time and justice to none. Only one man in that madness had the clarity and strength to pull out and say, no. Ten years later you realise Aamir has changed the system single-handedly. Every star now does only one film at a time, it's raised the quality bar of the entire industry.'

'It's true. Aamir has modernised filmmaking,' says cinematographer Ravi Chandran, who's shot films like *Black*, *Dil Chahta Hai*, *Paheli* and *Saawariya*. 'It's he who brought in sync sound as a producer, he who insisted on the discipline of written scripts and first ADs and contracts. He changed the ethos.'

Everyone is agreed *Lagaan*, Aamir's first film as a producer, was a watershed. More, it was an act of lunacy. A crew of 300 carted from Bombay to a one-horse town in the Bhuj desert for a six-month outdoor shoot. An entire village recreated in the harsh sand. And at a time when Bollywood is belting out its frothiest and most colour saturated formulas, 25 crore spent on a quixotic script, a rookie director, and a film that has no star cast, no costume change, no conventional romance, no villain, and speaks in Awadhi and English – languages untested on the Indian box-office. In hindsight it looks easy: success is a powerful negotiator: it commands sanction. Once *Lagaan* became an international hit, few needed to remember that Aamir floated his own production company to make the film because no other producer would back its harebrained magic. As Satyajit Bhatkal, long time friend and fellow sufferer from *Lagaan* says, 'Mad *hai, kuch bhi kar sakta hai*!'

Lagaan was singular in enabling a new imagination in Bollywood, redefining what a star or a hit film in a status quo industry could mean. But almost each of Aamir's films since has displayed a similar illogic in choice followed by unblinking commitment. *Lagaan* was followed by *Dil Chahta Hai* – unconventional slice of life film, ensemble cast, first-time director. Followed by a four-year hiatus and *Mangal Pandey* – a historical in the midst of chocolate NRI films, a low-octane director. Followed by *Rang De Basanti* – ensemble cast, fifth film on Bhagat Singh in recent time, and a director freshly emerged from a flop. 'Only a man of immense self-confidence could make such choices,' says Kunal Kohli, director of *Fanaa* (Aamir's only masala film in recent years), currently shooting a film in Bangkok with Rani and Saif. 'In an era of Raj and Rahul NRI films, in an industry where everyone airkisses and ass-licks, we need a man like Aamir who doesn't pamper anyone and never lowers his standards. He keeps things sane and level. Today, top filmmakers like Aditya Chopra, Karan Johar and Sanjay Leela Bhansali can get any star with a phone call, but no one can get Aamir without a script. It's beautiful. It's lovely to have a person like that.' 'He's swum miles and miles against the current, that's why we're talking about him today,' says Mehra. 'He's a fabulous entertainer yet when we look back, I think, his body of work is going to shine almost like a lonely star. He never judges directors by their flops and hits. He has the capacity to reach into the core and touch the nectar.'

With Aamir, touching the nectar can express itself in many ways. Refusing a coveted statue at Madame Tussauds'. Refusing to back down on the Narmada under threat from Modi. Stoically withstanding a call from Abu Salem years earlier. Or turning down a 35 crore deal from Adlabs now because they didn't have a script. When director Rakeysh Mehra ran into financial trouble before the start of *Rang De Basanti*, he sent him an SMS: Never fear. And waited five months without giving away the dates. 'Which star at the peak of his career would give two years of his life to a film,' says Ketan Mehta. Aamir had not cut his moustache or hair for months after *Mangal Pandey* was wrapped, waiting till Ketan felt he had the footage he needed. 'Producing a film like *Lagaan*, giving two years to *Mangal Pandey*, doing one film at a time – it takes great guts to do that and I think he's been revolutionary in that sense.'

'I don't intend it that way,' laughs Aamir, driving home late from a studio in Film City. He's deep in the entrails of his new film. The first print is a few days away and he's racing around town checking Dolby and colour and subtitles. He's just re-recorded a 60-piece string section live because the synth sound didn't satisfy him. (AR Rahman once laughed with amazement at Aamir's ability to locate an off-note in a track with 20 layers in it.) 'I listen to narrations as an audience, and I find myself attracted to the most off-beat scripts. Each time, I tell myself, Oh no! Not again! It can be very tiring to go with your belief. Lonely too. Once you're in though, you have to hold firm.'

More reflectively, he adds, 'I'm hungry for different things now. I want to make really quality films about important subjects – but in a completely mass entertainment space. Somehow I feel more courage to do that now without looking over my shoulder.' It's not just the gigantic box-office success of his choices that's responsible for this. In a curious way, the turmoil of his break-up from a seventeen-year marriage – civilised as it may have been – and living separately from his children, has honed him, moved him closer to who he really is, both in his work and his personal life. Adversity has a way of clarifying one's being. 'It made me more aware of myself, more sensitive to others,' says he. Kiran's companionship has completed the circle.

Aamir has always been a fiercely private man. In recent years, the media has feasted on unverified stories about him: an imminent break up with second wife, Kiran; supposed bitterness with his first wife, Reena; supposed cruelty to his ill brother, Faisal. He's often portrayed as an anal perfectionist, brilliant at his work but lacking in human warmth. Nothing could be further from the truth, say those who are close to him or have worked with him.

'People are completely wrong when they describe Aamir in terms of some "analysisparalysis",' says Prasoon Joshi, lyricist and CEO, McCann Erickson. 'He's a man who operates purely from heart and instinct. Everything else is post-rationalisation. I've worked with many stars,' he continues, 'and I can tell you, Aamir is the gold standard. He's a mirror in which other people have to square with themselves. He's a rare friend. A superstar who's not a megalomaniac. He's changed mainstream sensibility.' Even Karan Johar admits he has yet to make his own *Lagaan* or RDB.

'Two things drive Aamir,' agrees Kiran, 'passion and instinct. Both for people and work.' During the July floods of 2005, Aamir almost rode out on a bike to look for his ex-wife who could not be traced for a while. He has looked after his brother and father for years. He's widened the bed in his children's room so he can sleep with them when they come to stay over. He let actor Siddharth deliver the climax of RDB because he felt it suited his character better. These are the kind of humanising details Aamir will never voluntarily share in public. Add to that the fact that he never goes for any award functions; he's lashed out at the media for its celebrity obsession at the expense of primary duties; and he never graces supplements with gossipy interviews, and one has a sense of how precariously Aamir plays his stardom in a media saturated universe where success is often only as real as the perception of success.

Aamir cannot easily be drawn into cheap competitions, but as a close cousin says, 'Aamir loves to win.' So if you scratch hard enough, he will concede the media's superstar billings do grate on him sometimes. 'I make no money for them, so the media would like to scale me down from a superstar to a good character actor, a kind of Balraj Sahni,' says Aamir, chuckling ruefully. 'But star power is measured by a star's ability to draw crowds in the first week on the strength of his name alone. To measure that accurately you have to look at the numbers.'

The numbers always look splendid on Aamir. He commands astronomical rates: he will earn 25 crore from his fee and share-of-profit from his forthcoming film, *Gajini*. And every maverick film of his has earned the same if not more than the masala competition, including films like *Don*, *Krrish*, KANK, *Koi Mil Gaya*, *Main Hoon Na* and K3G. The thing to remember here, says Kohli, is that on one side there's only Aamir, risky scripts, and a host of unknown actors and directors. On the other, there's all the fire power of the industry. Star directors, multiple stars, powerful production houses, and tested formulas. Yet the numbers compare favourably. What's more, each time other superstars move away from their secure comfort zones, they falter. As Naseeruddin Shah says, 'Aamir is the only star I can think of who is not producing films only to make money. And the same directors have fallen flat when they have attempted similar films without him. That says a lot about him.'

'Perhaps a star should be measured by his flops,' says Aamir wickedly, confident in the knowledge that *Mangal Pandey* made about 18 crore in its first week, while hits like *Veer Zaara* made 17. But that's only a momentary wickedness. Truth is, Aamir and Shah Rukh represent two diametrically different impulses in the industry. Shah Rukh is the Dionysian principle: charisma, material flamboyance, and cheeky self-appropriations, endearing in their outrageousness. He does not challenge people, he fulfils their fantasy. He makes people comfortable because he allows them to coast in shallow waters: he is the magnified image of the world's hunger for razzle-dazzle luxury: its desire to work hard and live light. There's an honesty to that which has a charm of its own. It may not make for great cinema, but it creates great and crucial placebos.

Aamir represents something harder, more complex. He whispers to people about their better selves. His stardom lies in his craft, his deep, almost uncanny, acumen to reach for the heart of things. The mystique of Aamir is that he is an idealist in an industry that does not require him to be one. That's his magic move. And it pays rich dividends.

Drawing away from Aamir's house, a cab driver says, '*Is sheher mein bahut sitare dikhte hain, par is aadmi ko dekh ke dil khush ho jata hai. Bahut nek hain*. (This is a city full of stars, but seeing this man makes one's heart happy. There is such a clean sincerity about him.)' And purity can be very flamboyant. As Jaideep Sahni, scriptwriter, *Chak De*, says, 'In a cynical world, what can be more flamboyant emotionally for people than an important man who consistently stands by what he believes in. I'm certain Aamir's film will have great sensitivity coupled with a quiet aggression about what the film has to say, backed by the philosophy that nothing has the right to be boring.

TZP lives up to that. As Javed Akhtar says, '*Taare* has a minimal quality that only masters of their art can afford. They know how much is enough – you find this in actors like Brando and poets like Meer.' Writing about Aamir can be hazardous, because to ring true, every encomium needs a critical note, the black spot that will make it real. In Aamir's case, it's tough to find. He can be bull-headed, Mehra offers gamely. But that's a necessary trait. To hear the flute note.

Sonu Jain

Sonu Jain, 37, is working as a Consultant with the World Bank. She won the award while working with *The Indian Express.*

[There was a danger of India becoming a dumping ground for toxins – be it ships headed to the ship-breaking yards in Gujarat, unregulated imports of mercury and asbestos or just waste oil being shipped out from developed countries to be burnt here. While the rest of the world considered these as dangerous, India was in denial.]

TOLERATING TOXINS: MERCURY
Award-winning Story

Shivlings are making news once again – this time, not the ones made of ice but the ones made of metal, called 'parad shivlings', traded and installed in homes and temples across the country. Each of these has mercury as a key constituent, almost 30 per cent by weight – making this one of the most serious examples of uncontrolled mercury use in the country.

At a time when mercury is being phased out in the West because of its range of proven adverse effects on the central nervous system, India's imports of it have more than doubled in six years – from 254 tonnes in 1996-97 to 531 tonnes in 2002-03 – displacing US as the largest consumer of mercury in the world.

The US has a stringent regulatory system for mercury and is aggressively phasing out its use, but remains a key exporter to India. Spain is the largest exporter of mercury. What adds to the problem is the fact that there is no regulatory system in place in India. After 1992, mercury came under the Open General License which means any trader is free to import as much mercury as he wants. However, there is no inventory of where this mercury is going.

'In India, this trade is legal which is in contravention of the Basel Convention which prohibits trade of hazardous substances,' said Ravi Agarwal, director of the Delhi-based environment advocacy group Toxics Link, which has been tracking the mercury menace.

Experts say there are three main causes of concern:

- The gap between what is being imported (India imports all its mercury) and the known consumption. Last year, the Central Pollution Control Board asked the National Productivity Council to prepare an inventory. Nothing has been done.

- Increasing evidence of mercury in water and fish in several studies done by institutes and even by the government. A 1999 Calcutta University study of fish in the Hooghly found 1.18-1.20 mg per kg as compared to WHO's permissible level of 1 mg per kg.
- No official action plan.

Chlor-alkali plants, which make inputs for fertilizers and pesticides, are the single largest-known consumers of mercury, accounting for, as per official figures, 13 per cent of the imports.

Beyond this, is the large unregulated market of thermometer manufacturers and those which make thermostats, button cells and tubelights. Traders at Delhi's Tilak Bazaar, one of the largest mercury wholesale markets in the country, say their buyers are from a range of industries: ayurveda, paints and pesticides, temple and gurudwara builders, bangle makers, the cosmetic industry and, of course, shivling manufacturers.

After protests by NGOs, the government put pressure on the chlor-alkali industry to start replacing mercury with alternatives. 'We have taken a lead in bringing down our consumption by bringing in better technology,' said A Singh, president of the Chlor Alkali Manufacturing Association.

'Where is the 87 per cent of the mercury going? How is it being disposed? That is why mercury levels are so many times higher than WHO permissible limits,' said Chandra Bhushan, associate director, Centre for Science and Environment, who compiled a map of mercury hot-spots in the country.

What is worrying experts is the government's seeming indifference. Asked about studies that mercury spill from one thermometer can contaminate a 20-sq-km lake, secretary, environment and forest Prodipto Ghosh says he is not impressed.

'If mercury was so dangerous, I would not be alive today,' he says. A chemical engineer by training, he says he has handled mercury. 'We will not spend so much money in replacing mercury when the same money can be used for more pressing environmental concerns ... We need our own studies to see if it is that injurious to health.'

However, he admits that there is too much mercury coming in and there is no inventory. 'We have asked for more studies, we will decide after due scientific diligence,' he said.

Why Mercury is Dangerous

Evidence from the world

Japan's Minamata Tragedy (1956), where 12,000 were affected after eating mercury-poisoned fish set off an international campaign against its use. Several global studies have concluded that mercury has:

• Neuro-toxic effects: on muscle coordination, behaviour, even memory

• Hampers nerve conduction after long-term occupational exposure

• Renal failure

• Chronic exposure can impair fertility and pregnancy.

In India

• Environment Secretary says there is no evidence of any damage, need to conduct our own studies

• 'By the time, studies are done, it may be too late,' says Bharat Sagar of the environmental medicine group at LNJP Hospital in New Delhi. 'We do not even have the knowhow to test people for mercury contamination. They are treated as routine neurological disorder cases.'

Personal Account

My quest to get to the nub of the mercury muddle began one morning in the general ward of St Stephens hospital, one of the oldest hospitals in Delhi. They were among the first to work towards phasing out thermometers and blood pressure monitors that contained mercury.

I watched a fascinating drill. A thermometer fell 'accidentally', and little silver globules skittered about on the floor. The staff, all in white tunics, quickly drew the globules into syringes, and flushed them into a jar filled with water. They were to be sold back to the thermometer company.

It was clear that the hospital was convinced that mercury was dangerous and had to be handled gingerly.

In the next few minutes, accompanied by Express photographer Premnath Pandey, I was in a cycle-rickshaw on my way to Tilak Bazaar in Chandni Chowk, one of the largest wholesale markets in India. I had learnt that mercury was sold in bulk there and it was important to find out who the buyers were.

Soon, I was in a bustling lane that sold every possible metal and chemical. The shops all looked tiny and lacklustre, displaying a small sample of their wares. Inside, there were warehouses. After a few inquiries, I was directed to a wholesale shop of mercury. From a place where every globule was handled with kid-gloves, I was in a place where caskets were being lifted and transported with no protection whatsoever. Fortuitously, the owner of the shop turned out to be a distant relative. He led us to his warehouse lined with dozens of metal jars containing mercury. When I asked him if he knew how hazardous mercury was, he dismissed it as a fancy Western idea and urged me to have another 'cold drink' instead. The only important clue I managed to elicit from him was that some of the largest customers were chlor-alkali factories, makers of Ayurvedic medicine and, surprisingly, those who made shivlings for temples. Many shivlings, which are symbols of Lord Shiva of the Hindu pantheon, had 30 per cent mercury by weight.

This trader was not the only one who thought I was making a mountain out of a mercury molehill. The then secretary, Ministry of Environment and Forest, told me how he handled mercury in labs as a chemical engineer and 'I am still alive'. The question posed to him was what he thought of India putting millions at risk by increasing consumption of mercury manifold in the last decade (India is the second largest consumer of mercury). This was when all over the world it had been proven that its unregulated use and exposure could lead to damage of the brain and the nervous system. Several countries in the West, including the USA, was phasing it out.

Mercury, commonly used in thermometers, paints, fluorescent lamps and industrial chemicals, is not mined in India. Imports of mercury, mostly from Spain, Britain, the United States, Russia and the Netherlands, had almost doubled in a decade. Despite the warnings from several NGOs like Toxics Link, mercury was still under Open General licence and there was no inventory of the exports coming in. The scientific diligence that the government talked of was being done for years but with no conclusive results.

In many similar stories on mercury, asbestos, or PCBs where science does not establish a direct link between exposure to metals and a particular disease, I found ample scope for vested interest to doubt and discard whatever little evidence one had.

As a journalist trying to get to the bottom of it, I was putting the pieces of a complex jigsaw together. There were clues in some of the evidence submitted in the numerous court cases, the victims themselves who had been fighting corporations to pay them compensation, the few doctors who actually spent their time researching them, the bureaucrats who were supposed to be doing scientific diligence and the people whose livelihoods depended on the trade of hazardous metal.

It was complex and entangled and probably beyond the scope of government studies that often looked at the issue from a single perspective.

In the same week I had a meeting with a doctor who was trying to find that elusive link between a patient who was suffering from lung cancer or TB and his exposure to either mercury or asbestos. Dr TK Joshi told me why his job was such a challenge. It was always too late by the time most of the patients were diagnosed with TB or related complications. The tests that needed to be done to establish a direct link to their exposures were often expensive and time-consuming. Most patients died before they could be done. He led me to Mangabhai Patel in Gujarat who was suffering from mesothelioma, a form of lung cancer he contracted from prolonged exposure to asbestos in a power plant in Gujarat. He was a rare one who had actually managed to get a small compensation. There are 500 case histories that have been submitted to the Supreme Court on a PIL that asks for a ban on the use, import and manufacture of asbestos. There are others who die quietly.

In Mangabhai's case, the Ahmedabad-based National Institute of Occupational Health had worked diligently to conclude he was suffering from asbestos-related illnesses. Most normal hospitals are not even equipped to diagnose the disease. If the disease is not proven, the industries never have to pay compensation.

It was punitive litigation that brought down consumption of asbestos in the US to 2 per cent of what it was twenty years ago. In the same time, the industry coughed up $11 million on mesothelioma litigation involving 600,000 claims.

India is the only country in the world where consumption of asbestos is increasing by 12 per cent each year as it imports a large chunk of what is produced in the world. Yet, the clean-up is still to begin, making it the most attractive place for newer asbestos units.

There was a similar callousness, denial and status quo in several other instances that I had a chance of investigating: dirty ships lined with asbestos landing at Alang, hazardous oil waste lying in several of our ports, and toxins in paints and toys.

In the name of development and growth, was India becoming the happy dumping ground for the world? The most common argument for lack of enforcing existing regulation or formulating new ones was that the poor would be deprived of livelihood. The ship-breaking yards of Alang have been the most vocal.

Or is it that India had more pressing problems? Asbestos, lead and mercury were peripheral issues?

There were some no-brainers on regulation which the government refused to see even as they tried to look for concrete evidence on these hazardous substances. Take the waste oil that lay on many of the Indian ports. By the time the oil was tested, it was always more than 30 days, a period within which a consignment can be sent back to the exporting country if found to be hazardous. If you cross those 30 days, you live with it.

Or in Alang, where several workers at the ship-breaking yard had accidents as they were exposed to chemicals because there was a lack of safety regulation. They often cut through asbestos and other metals with their bare hands, without the basic masks and gloves.

It struck me that several of these measures could be implemented irrespective of the debate on science. It made common sense even if the Basel Convention that India is signatory to does not make sense to regulators as yet.

Personally, the jigsaw when pieced together, left very little doubt on the need to act and that too, soon.

Sreenivasan Jain

Sreenivasan Jain, 41, is
Managing Editor, NDTV 24x7.

[Sreenivasan Jain witnesses the dramatic transformation in the nature of elections, politics, politicians, and more profoundly, in the manner in which the business of politics has come to be conducted.]

WHY THE MEDIA SHOULD WAKE UP THE NEW POLITICAL OLIGARCHY

Personal Account

In the dying weeks of the campaign for the 2008 Karnataka assembly elections, I went to visit a senior Congress observer camping at an anonymous guest house in Bangalore. A set of large, grey, hard-shell VIP suitcases were stacked in a corner of the room. 'They don't want it,' he said, shrugging his shoulders in bemusement. The suitcases contained cash despatched from Delhi, in a time-honoured practice of the high command supplementing the expenses of its local candidates.

Earlier, a Karnataka Congress functionary had taken me over a set of confidential excel sheets to explain the methodology used to dispense the cash: based on the candidate's economic status, winnability, sub-region, rival candidate, etc. The high command typically offered anywhere from Rs 5-10 lakh to a maximum of Rs 25-30 lakh per candidate, per election. But in Karnataka, in 2008, virtually none of the candidates wanted the central 'donation'. They were probably spending that amount daily. Till today there are no exact figures of how much money was collectively thrown around in that election, but conservative estimates suggest the average expenditure per constituency ranged from Rs 60-80 crore. A survey conducted by the Centre for Media Studies, released a year later, confirmed what any of us who were in Bangalore in the closing weeks of April 2008 already knew: that the Karnataka elections had witnessed the worst abuse of money power, more than of any other Indian state.

On the day of the results, we had the Chief Election Commissioner N Gopalaswami on NDTV. He said he was shocked by the amount of 'filthy lucre' sloshing around. As it turned out, the Karnataka results were widely reported as a 'watershed', not a dubious watershed of monetary excess but a political watershed: the BJP's first government in South India. In itself, this represents the disconnect between the new and old forms of politics, in some ways, a disconnect of perception and emphasis, out of step with the dramatic transformation in the nature of elections, politics (and politicians), and more profoundly, in the manner in which the business of politics has come to be conducted. In the case of Karnataka, as it subsequently emerged, the BJP's win, and the consolidation of their wafer-thin majority by the 'acquisition' of MLAs from other parties, was, to a large part, powered by a secular catalyst: mining money.

I began my career in journalism in 1995 with NDTV. Looking back, the calendar of that first reporting year was an itinerary that reflected the high-voltage political instability of the times: in October I was in Gujarat, staking out a farmhouse in Vasania, a small village on the outskirts of Ahmedabad where Shankarsinh Vaghela had ring-fenced rebel BJP MLAs with whom he proposed to overthrow Chief Minister Keshubhai Patel. A few months earlier, I had been outside the Viceroy Hotel in Hyderabad, the epicentre for Chandrababu Naidu's infamous coup against his father-in-law NT Rama Rao. Then, there were the fragmented mandates of the Lok Sabha elections of 1996 and 1998, triggering weeks of messy, chaotic government-formation. Much of the action unfolded around the state bhawans, which became centres of intrigue, power-broking and, in the case of Andhra Bhawan, tasty thali meals. Those were heady, oddly innocent times compared to the jaw-dropping rise of the new corporatised politics (and politician).

The corralling of MLAs, overnight coup de états, the hustling back and forth between Raj Bhawan and party headquarters, the mysterious movement of letters of support: however venal and grubby, these were the kinds of political transactions which we had the vocabulary and the tools to grasp and report, down to every mind-boggling detail. All this unruly activity made up the jigsaw pieces which collectively shaped the wider narratives of contemporary Indian politics. If we were, to borrow a cliché, scripting the first draft of history, then this was a ground-eye view of a history of sorts: the rise of regional forces, coalitions at the Centre, the mainstreaming of the Hindu right.

What we missed was the silent, but no less dramatic enrichment of our political class: the rise of the builder-developer-equityholding politician-cum-stakeholder, which has over the past decade come to jeopardize the democratic enterprise, some would say, beyond repair.

Why is the rise of the new politics a media blind spot? For one, the old fashioned business of 'power' politics: the internal struggles of a political party, the ever-shifting circles of loyalty and disfavour which still form the bulk of mainstream political journalism, is more interesting. (It is also easily reportable: this is 'revealed' politics, played out in the open, or which has well-worn routes to allow even its more opaque aspects to be made public). For all my exposure, from the vantage position that Mumbai offers to the Munnabhai-as-CEO phenomenon, I confess I still warm to the old school of political reportage: tracing, for instance the implosion of the BJP, the intrigue and hi jinks that have inevitably marked the search for a new party president, the poring over every word of the RSS sarsanghachalak's press conference (when he said 'change is good', did he mean Advani should go?) and so on. But these old fashioned tools that we still use to decode the modern political matrix threaten to be rendered hollow by the new politics.

There have been several early warnings of this change, stretching back a decade, notably to a 1999 survey by the Centre for Study of Developing Societies (CSDS), which, commissioned to map the changing social and economic profile of state assemblies and Parliament, found that 70 per cent of MLAs and MPs belonged to the 'rich' or 'super-rich' categories. Today, a third of the members of Parliament's Standing Committee on Industry are businessmen. The Standing Committee on Finance counts amongst its members a venture capitalist, two regional media barons, and an industrialist. The Public Accounts Committee has big-ticket contractors in its ranks.

Another reason for the media blind spot is the turgid legacy of 'scam' journalism, a genre which reached its high noon in the mid-to-late nineties, and to which I had an intense and brief exposure. In between staking out Andhra Bhawan, I found myself doing double duty outside CBI HQ, the rather squalid offices of the Enforcement Directorate behind New Delhi's Khan

Market, and the Tis Hazari courts. At any given point, the lawyers, the accused, and the sundry supporting cast-members of any of the following 'scams' could appear at these locations, sometimes more than one group on the same day: Bofors (the first set of Swiss bank documents had been returned in 1997), the hawala scandal, the Sukh Ram / telecom scam, the fodder scam. Each scandal had a brief, sensational turn on the national centre stage before vanishing in a haze of botched investigations and flimsy evidence. Some of these scams would witness an occasional resurrection because of some belated legal development, prompting editorials on how Indians have lost interest in corruption. Even if this national ennui with corruption is somewhat overstated (the Naxals, for instance, seem to be very interested in the subject), there are some merits to the argument: the Great Indian Scam in the classical sense of the term, carries an anachronistic whiff, a remnant of pre-liberalised India, with its own tedious, clerical vocabulary: 'acts of omission and commission', 'sabotaging the legal process', 'causing loss to the exchequer', 'assets disproportionate to known sources of income'. But the act of political enrichment, ever creative, ever mutating, has followed the arc of a globalising economy. It's no longer about the rigging of the tender process to favour a predetermined bidder. It's more likely that the minister and the bidder are the same party. No longer the 'gift' of an apartment in Dubai's Jumeirah Beach, when the recipient is probably a joint partner in the same real estate project. A secret deposit in a Cayman Islands account for allowing a port or an SEZ? Not any more. How much better to buy up all the land in and around the project in advance under a newly floated company and then sell it at a 300 per cent mark up to the developer? Bit by bit, the levers of power, money and politics have converged to create a set of linkages that are paradoxically both wide-ranging and invisible. For the media to claim boredom, futility or simply a lack of analytical tools as reasons for this invisibility is to ignore the elephant in the room.

There is a more immediate risk, quite apart from editorial abdication, in ignoring the rise of the new political oligarchy. We need to look no further than the ground beneath our feet. Every time another inch of pavement is swallowed up, or a park, municipal school or public maidan gets converted into an apartment block, or an entire neighborhood is opened up for redevelopment, it is the impact – direct or covert – of the new politics. We can be thoroughly uninterested in the provenance of our councillors, MLAs or MPs, but to then express anguish at the slow choking of our living habitat is entirely disingenuous. This is nowhere truer than in Mumbai, in the recent elections. Hours of airtime and pages went into reporting the antics of Raj Thackeray the Rabble Rouser. But did we spend enough time reporting the antecedents of Raj the Builder? Raj Thackeray may be persona non-grata at Matoshree, the official Thackeray residence, but he is a board member of Matoshree Infrastructure, his real estate company. (What an extraordinarily persuasive calling card in Mumbai's dog-eat-dog real estate market! 'Matoshree Infrastructure calling. We would like to discuss taking over your old building.') For several years, through gentle and not so gentle persuasion, this fortuitously (or ominously)-named establishment has developed properties all over the city, several of them in the Marathi heartland of Dadar-Shivaji Park, fuelling that area's real estate boom, and out-pricing, in several instances, the very same Maharashtrian middle class that Raj Thackeray claims to represent in his other avatar as a political demagogue.

Raj's thriving parallel career of course remained largely unreported, until Matoshree Infrastructure, backed by a consortium, acquired the defunct Kohinoor Mills in Dadar for a staggering Rs 421 crore in 2005. Also part of the consortium: the Kohinoor Group, owned by Manohar Joshi, a known Uddhav loyalist. The purchase took place a year before Raj Thackeray's exit from the Shiva Sena, but the Raj-Joshi business partnership endured even after their political rift. When the consortium was hit by recession and poor business strategy earlier this year, it exited the deal. They made, if market sources are to be believed, a tidy Rs 300 crore (Matoshree officials insist its only Rs 60 crore). As the voice of a dispossessed Marathi underclass, Raj the Demagogue may have benefited from the recession. As it turned out, Builder Raj didn't too badly either, reinforcing the basic credo of the new politics: there are no real enemies. Everyone wins, no one loses.

It could be argued that even if every single detail of Raj

Thakceray's commercial interests had been vigorously tracked down, scrutinised in detail to sift the legal from the illegal, and the findings widely reported, it may have made no difference, in today's climate, to his public standing. The ethical matrix of socialist India may be skewered for its hypocrisies, but it's still hard to imagine whether ten years ago we would have cheered with the same vigour the entrepreneurial successes of our MPs, MLAs, and ministers, the expressions 'conflict' and 'interest' so blithely forgotten as civil aviation ministers pose with airline owners and oil ministers count as their bosom buddies petrochemical barons. Perhaps no one embodied better the new Teflon-coated politics of post-liberalised India better than the late YS Rajashekhar Reddy. Despatched, in 2009, to Andhra Pradesh to report on the funeral and the political aftermath of the death of YSR, I followed the route taken by his remains from Kurnool airfield to Hyderabad's Begumpet airport. In the duration of this brief helicopter ride, YSR had acquired near-canonical status. Statues were being planned, districts were to be renamed, a biopic was announced, and so was, naturally, a YSR temple. Simultaneously, Hyderabad was abuzz with the number of deals – pending and current, legal and benami – which ran the risk of jeopardy because of his sudden demise. These contradictory responses bore testimony to YSR's success in combining grassroots populism and mass appeal with a semi-corporate superstructure of mine owners, wealthy farmers, real estate barons and big-project contractors. It is the kind of politician – as – CEO-cum-folk-hero strategy that has been refined with varying success in India's better developed South and the West, and is now gaining ground everywhere. In this he shared more than a common vision with Sharad Pawar, long held as the benchmark of India's political oligarchs. Like Pawar, YSR's clever positioning as an emancipator-in-chief immunised him to the constant accusations of corruption and wealth amassment, which, for YSR, towards the final stages of the 2009 election campaign had reached near mythic levels. When the results were declared, and YSR coronated, one could not but feel somewhat sympathetic to Chandrababu Naidu who deluged journalists with pamphlets that outlined, in eye-watering detail, the various malpractices of the Congress regime, all of which he claimed led to the YSR family's personal wealth multiplying from Rs 41 lakh to Rs 10,000 crore.

This is not to say that digging the dirt doesn't yield victories, however minor – as we discovered in Goa in 2006, alerted by the vigorous public activism against the new Regional Plan, which activists claimed was 'selling off' of Goa to builders and politicians. Goa, of course, was already a mess, even before the protests erupted. Hire a driver with sound local knowledge for a trip down north Goa's Golden Mile (more like 6 miles) from Candolim to Anjuna and you will be quickly brought up to date with why this idyllic stretch now resembles Delhi's Lajpat Nagar: 'this is Narayan Rane's hotel', 'this is so-and-so MLA's mall', and so on. The Regional Plan, claimed Goa's citizenry, was going to precipitate the crisis beyond repair. Our team of reporters spent weeks matching arcane references in land records with actual construction sites, squatting behind shrubbery or wading through mangroves to secretly film illegal hotels and apartment buildings. The paper trail was enormous: this was, as is the norm nowadays, a bipartisan act of fraudulence, stretching across various wings of the government and cutting across political parties. By the fourth week, we had enough documentary evidence to establish the massive scale of malfeasance: of how the Regional Plan had violated almost every single zoning law and safeguard to parcel off prime forest, coastal and hilltop areas to develop resorts, IT Parks, townships, hotels, and something inexplicably called a Techno Recreational Centre.

The pinning down of political culpability was trickier: the plan had been drafted by the Town and Planning Minister Babush Monserrat, but he legitimately grumbled that it was wrong to make him the sole scapegoat. As we widened the net, we found, for instance, that a large number of real estate firms had been floated by the chief minister's son, several in the name of his wife, in the run up to the release of the Regional Plan, and that some of these companies had purchased land which the Plan had marked for commercial development. Animating a swindle of this scale for TV viewers is always a challenge, but one inadvertent photo-op, when Babush drove us through a road he had newly cut across a paddy field, which, he explained, took ten minutes off his the trip from his official home in Talegaon to his spanking new house on Miramar Beach, proved to be the tipping point. The story broke, Babush resigned, and the plan was scrapped. In the elections that followed (another high-spending extravaganza, almost rivaling Karnataka), Babush won as an independent, and was promptly inducted into the government. But all was not lost. Goa is now debating a fresh Regional Plan, which many hope is less likely to be as devastating as the earlier one. Illegal construction has resumed, with less vigour. And Babush couldn't get Town and Planning portfolio. He was made education minister, confining him to a position from which he is investigating the contamination of mid-day meals.

No one understands the significance of incremental gains better than the Association of Democratic Reforms (ADR), which through National Election Watch, a network of more than 1,200 non-governmental associations, has introduced a sort of real-time dimension to the burgeoning fortunes of our elected representatives through the publicising of the contents of their affidavits before elections. ADR's first victory, which went up to the Supreme Court, was to make the filing of these affidavits mandatory. Each ADR press conference is only a depressing reiteration of something we now know: that the election in any constituency in India is becoming a choice between, say, two builders. ADR and its constituents are now hoping that this crushing non-choice, presented as a fait accompli by political parties under the euphemism of 'winnability', would be vigorously questioned, and may eventually lead the parties to consider other factors beyond bank balance (for instance, good performance. Now there's an idea). The signs are not encouraging. The media has yet to fully recalibrate its sights to analyse politics from the prism of rampant corporatisation. And political parties seem to wake up to the perils of encouraging the oligarchs in their ranks only when they bite back, like the BJP's recent experience in Karnataka with the Reddy brothers, and for the Congress with Jagan Reddy and his supporters in Andhra Pradesh. Until then, at a micro level of which elections are fought, it is a terrible narrowing of democratic options. At a larger level, the implications of the shaping of policy at the hands of politicians heavily compromised by their own financial interests.

Of course, there will also be a relatively minor dilemma of what to do with the unspent cash, dispatched by the Centre, but rejected by its high-spending local candidates. What will happen to this money, I asked the Congress leader in Bangalore, gesturing towards the suitcases. Where will this go? I don't know, he said, half-jokingly. Perhaps Jharkhand?

Subrata Nagchoudhary

Subrata Nagchoudhary is Resident Editor, *The Indian Express*, Kolkata.

[Visits to the villages involved in the Nandigram clashes brought out tales of the gruesome atrocities committed by the state's forces and the Opposition.]

AN INCONVENIENT TRUTH FOR SECULAR CPM: NANDIGRAM VICTIMS' MAINLY MUSLIM FACE

Award-winning Story

'The first fallout of what has happened at Nandigram is that it weakens our case in Gujarat. The CPM, which always speaks of high ideals, is indulging in such shameful acts of violence. This is not an issue that concerns Muslims only. It's a national issue.'
Kamal Faruqui, permanent member, All India Muslim Personal Law Board

'The only good thing with regard to Muslims is that in the last 30 years of Left rule in West Bengal, they were safe. What happened in Nandigram now puts question mark on that, too.'
Manzoor Alam, general secretary, All India Milli Council

This is, perhaps, the worst kept secret of the Nandigram violence that's now being talked about openly. It is also an embarrassment for the CPM which swears by its secular credentials: a majority of those targeted by its party cadres as they reclaim their turf are Muslim.

Certainly, the violence is political, not communal – the protests were over proposed land acquisition and a turf war, not any religious issue – but the demographics of Nandigram and the nature of opposition to the CPM have ensured that wherever you go, in relief camp after relief camp, most of the refugees are Muslim.

Local administration officials admit that at least 65 per cent of those huddled in the largest relief camp at the Brojomohan Tiari Institute are Muslim. So is the victim of the first gang rape case officially registered and eight of those who have been killed so far.

Then there is the reference the National Human Rights Commission (NHRC) has made to Gujarat in its indictment of the Bengal state government. Ironically, the CPM, at pains to draw a distinction between Gujarat and Nandigram, has ended up by reinforcing this aspect.

Ask CPM MP Mohammed Salim and he says this is a mere coincidence. 'Those who are trying to draw the Gujarat-Nandigram parallel are trying to undermine the seriousness of the Gujarat riots. If a particular area has a 46 per cent Muslim population it is natural that they will also be affected.'

When contacted, Abdus Sattar, minister of state for minorities welfare and development and madrassa education, said, 'A large number of Muslims might have been affected but what happened in Nandigram was not on the basis of religion. The Chief Minister is the minister for minorities. I have no other comment to make.'

What both the MP and the minister do not admit is that sections in the party are concerned over a possible backlash given how a majority of the victims in Nandigram are Muslim.

Consider the following:

• In areas where the government proposed land acquisition for the chemical SEZ, almost 65 per cent of the population is Muslim, largely the middle peasantry and share-croppers. Said Siddiqullah

Though the violence in Nandigram is political, not communal, the Muslims are the worst affected.

Chowdhury of Jamiat-e-Ulema-Hind which became the backbone of the political opposition. 'We could mobilise Muslims because they are the ones most dependent on land for their livelihood. Most of them are unrecorded sharecroppers haunted by the fear that they might not get any compensation for not possessing valid documents. In the core area of the proposed SEZ, a large number of Muslims owned small shops and were engaged in tailoring and zari work.'

It's no surprise that the top rung of the Bhoomi Uchched Pratirodh Committee (Save Land Committee) – the umbrella group that began the agitation against the CPM – is Muslim: the chief is Abu Sufiyan, a former CPM panchayat leader who the party claims was expelled because of alleged financial irregularities. Sufiyan, however, claims, he fell out of favour because he 'refused to carry out illegal orders'.

The working president of the BUPC is Abdus Samad who owes his allegiance to the Congress. Helping Sufiyan and Samad are Abu Taher of the Trinamool Congress; Ashrafultullah who is the treasurer; and executive committee member Sayum Kazi.

Muslims make up a significant section of the villages in Nandigram's Block 1 – the core of the agitation – which include Muhammadpur, Kendamarichar, Jalpai, Samsabad, Daudpur, Kalicharanpur, Garchakrebaria and Satengabad-Ranichawk.

Admits Block Development Officer Ashok Sarkar: 'In most of these villages, a large number of houses damaged belong to Muslims. They were from both sides but obviously those under the BPUC banner have suffered more.' One estimate, according to Samad, is that in the latest cycle of violence, 500 houses belonging to Muslims have either been burnt or damaged.

While the CPM may see in these facts nothing more than mere coincidence, several powerful, influential voices from the Muslim community – and the Opposition – are now speaking up.

Says pro-CPM Salman Khurshid, secretary, Muslim Institute, a highly respected organisation of Muslim intellectuals: 'Muslims in the state are thoroughly frustrated at what happened in Nandigram. The High Court has also called it (the March 14 firing) unconstitutional. It was just like in Gujarat where Narendra Modi gave his men three days to wrap up their operation. In Nandigram, CPM cadres were let loose from 6 to 9 November when the

After the 14 March police firing many people were forced to move to relief camps.

administration collapsed. The Muslims in the state have been saying that there is no difference between BJP and the so called progressive Marxists.'

Wrote *Akhbar-e-Mashriq*, the largest Urdu newspaper in Kolkata: 'Believers of Marxist philosophy have never accepted democracy by heart. For remaining in power they can resort to any cruelty and oppression and term those as legally valid. Both the BJP and the CPM intend to make common people mental slaves to attain their goal … For God's sake, Buddhadeb Bhattacharjee, let the (CRPF) jawans do their work, and issue instructions to the CPM cadres to return to their barracks.'

The respected *Azad Hind* also wrote on 15 November: 'In this tense and dirty ambience at present, everybody should remain cautious because power's toxicity can put any one on the wrong path. Specially, Muslim organisations and the Muslim people need to take steps keeping in mind the prevailing situation.'

Next to Nandigram firing site, CPM men were holed up with arms, ammo: CBI

The CPM-led Left Front government in West Bengal has maintained that the 14 March police firing in Nandigram in which fourteen people were killed was 'unfortunate' and 'tragic' and that the police had little choice when they were faced with a violent mob.

The government denied that CPM party cadres were in any way involved.

However, in what could deeply embarrass the government, the Central Bureau of Investigation (CBI) – ordered by the Calcutta High Court to probe the incident – has found evidence that establishes a link between the violence that day and CPM cadres who were supplied illegal arms and ammunition.

Highly placed sources have told the *Sunday Express* that the CBI's report contains evidence to show how well before the incident in Nandigram on 14 March, party cadres were brought in by local CPM leaders and accommodated in 'three office rooms' of the Janani Brick Field at Sherkhanchawk, barely 300 m from the Bhangabera bridge, the site of the police firing.

Three days after the incident, the CBI arrested ten of those CPM cadre members during a surprise raid on the kiln. Based on their interrogation and recovery of material, the CBI has claimed that those arrested were supplied illegal weapons and a huge cache of ammunition by an 'organised political party' (a reference to the CPM) with a view to create terror and attack 'political activists of the opposite political party at the point of gun and muscle power'.

The stockpile included .315 rifles, country-made firearms, shotguns, automatic pistols, revolvers and hundreds of cartridges.

Raj Kanojia, a spokesman of the state police, confirmed that the police force deployed in Nandigram on that day did not use .315 cartridges. But, significantly, the CBI team found as many as '238 pieces of empty cartridge case of 8 mm/.315 from the men arrested at the brick kiln.'

The CBI team also reported that those arrested had as many as 367 pieces of live cartridges of this 8 mm/.315 variety. Some of the cartridges recovered were said to be blood-stained.

Five mobile phone handsets were recovered from the arrested men in the brick kiln. The CBI is said to be investigating the calls made to and from these phones. Sources said the agency has established that the cadre members were in touch with local leaders, including gun-runners and local criminals.

CBI investigators also recovered, from those arrested, several books of CPM party receipts, leaflets of the party's youth wing, Democratic Youth Federation, and the All India Krishak Sabha, the party's peasant wing. Figuring in the list of items recovered:

'CPM flags, telephone diaries, personal diaries, green helmets, correspondence, a map and some yellow plastic gunny bags having blackish stains.'

Benoy Konar, CPM state secretariat and central committee member and the president of the West Bengal unit of the All India Krishak Sabha, when asked about this evidence said: 'Our party men in Nandigram needed to protect themselves from the onslaught of the rival camps. We will have our defence should the issue come up before the court.'

The CBI's finding reinforces public apprehension in Nandigram that the area is set for a protracted, even violent, political turf battle. Seizing on land as an issue, rival political parties have got together and forced the CPM onto the defensive.

Many CPM voters among the block of villagers who refused to join the protests against the government's decision to set up a chemical hub in Nandigram, have been evicted from their homes. State Industries Minister Nirupam Sen admitted that the party had been 'caught on the wrong foot' as it could not reach out to the villagers in time.

Although Chief Minister Buddhadeb Bhattacharjee has announced that there will be no hub – and, therefore, no land acquisition – in Nandigram, the region is still tense and those evicted from their homes are increasingly impatient.

What CBI says it found from the ten men arrested

Arms

- .315 rifle having SL NO. AB 846231
- .315 rifle having SL No. AB 002231
- .315 rifle having SL No. AB 002312
- .315 rifle having SL NO. AB 000041
- Country-made firearm (rifle) without any number.
- Shotgun, made in England, No 26847, single-barreled
- Shotgun with serial No 527932, single-barreled
- Firearm with the impression DBS Enterprise, Calcutta (India), model 55
- Shotgun with impression 'Selected Forged Steel Proof', 2 ¾ inch chamber, model 94C
- Country-made pistol
- Automatic pistol made in China
- Country-made six-cylinder revolver

- One revolver made in Japan
- Country-made pistol

Ammunition
- 238 empty cartridge cases of 8 mm /.315 bore
- 47 live .12 bore cartridges
- 27 live .12 bore cartridges and one empty case
- 44 live cartridges of various types
- 33 live cartridges of various type
- 367 live cartridges of 8 mm/.315
- 261 live cartridges of .380 inch bore, and one empty case

Swati Thiyagarajan

Swati Thiyagaraj, 38, is Senior Special Correspondent, NDTV 24x7. She hosts her own show 'Bornwild'.

[Wild elephants and tribals are locked in battle in the Keonjhar area of Orissa. Due to mining, the Elephant corridor has been shut off.]

LAST CHANCE
Personal Account

In fifteen years of reporting on wildlife and conservation I had never seen anything like what I saw in Orissa's Kheonjhar district.

Every night that we were there, the tribals and elephants were in conflict. We would drive from village to village and see ravaged homes, fields and roads. We also saw dead elephants and dead people.

How did a place, once home to some of the most dense saal forests with the largest number of the eastern population of the Asiatic Elephant in India become their graveyard? Nine elephants were electrocuted and killed the month that we were there and over 100 elephants went missing from the census count. The nine were killed by locals with electric wires while the missing elephants were killed by poachers.

For the local communities the elephant had become a nightmare. I spent a day in a village where twenty-two of the twenty-three houses were destroyed by the elephants and the tribals slept in a cave in a nearby hill, too terrified to sleep in their homes.

At harvest time the elephant herds simply kick their way into homes in search of the stored grain. Hundreds of mining operations have destroyed the existing elephant corridors forcing them to move into new areas.

Elephants, as a herd, are lead by a female, the matriarch. She leads the herd through time-tested paths that the herd has used for decades. Her memory tells her where to look for food and water. When these migratory corridors are destroyed, the herds are in disarray. Elephants need close to 200 litre of water and 200 kg of

Tribals and elephants are in constant conflict due to human population encroaching on to elephant territory.

food every day to survive. The devastated habitat, the pollution and the sludge are starving them out of the forests and they have begun to focus on the agricultural fields for their food.

The elders of the community had loved and revered the animal. They had worshipped it. Elephants and people lived in harmony for decades with the occasional mishap of a male tusker killing a person or damaging property. Today, it is a nightly phenomenon.

In the ten days that I spent in Kheonjhar, elephants raided the villages every night. People stayed awake out of fear, lining the roads and waiting for the forest department to come and help them. I saw herds of elephants with their young, come out of the forest for raids in broad daylight. This was an indication of their desperation. I also saw crowds of people follow the herds, get in their way, hurl stones and sticks at them.

Only a fool would deny that excessive mining of this area has created the problem. Many other reasons were given to us by the local administration. We were told that the slash and burn agriculture practiced by some of the tribals was to blame for the escalating conflict. We were told that a growing human population was encroaching onto the elephant territory. We were told that the elephant population had grown larger and that they were leaving the forests. No one could say why the conflict had started just a decade ago; as all the above-mentioned reasons had always existed and yet somehow elephants and people seemed to have co-existed well.

Ten years ago the boom in Orissa's mining industry began. The prices of steel and iron ore almost doubled in the time and the state decided to cash in.

I would love to live in an ideal world and ban all mining, but that is not my world. It would also be hugely hypocritical of me to take a stand and ask for a mining ban when I live in the city in a high-rise apartment and drive a car. If I could do without steel and iron I would.

Mining is a necessary evil unless we change our world; meanwhile, at least we can ensure responsible practices with least impact on the environment. The problem is the lack of transparency in the process and a lack of social responsibility in the industry. Let us also not forget the huge illegal mining racket. Barely any environment assessments were conducted before mining leases were given out. No assessments were made of the elephant corridors and no efforts made to prevent the shocking pollution. As I walked through the forests I could see the trees covered in black grime and small streams and rivulets choked with sludge.

This area is also the catchment for the Brahmini and Baitharini rivers, lifelines that flow through Orissa. The Brahmini and Baitharini also power the last of the remaining mangroves, estuaries and systems of Bitherkanika. Bitherkanika is the second largest mangrove swamp in India, a highly important ecosystem whose water comes from these two rivers that will get polluted and diverted for mining activities. If these rivers get choked, over exploited and if their catchment areas are destroyed, it will spell the death of vast ecosystems for Orissa and jeopardize the survival of the people in the state.

I also saw large tracts of forests that had been hacked down not just to set up the steel processing plants or destroyed by mining but to build the chassis of the trucks used to transport the steel and iron ore to the port. On being questioned, the mining minister told me that it was not his problem and that it was up to the forest department to sort out the issue and that the state needed development.

People and elephants died in the conflict. Yet not a single politician had bothered to visit the area. The Chief Minister, Naveen Patnaik told me that his government was doing all it could to make sure that forests and wildlife were not affected and when asked if he had visited the area he said that he would look into the matter.

Government records show that 301 people have been killed by elephants and over 380 elephants have been killed since 2003.

Elephants are moving away from their range areas and spreading across the state creating conflict and fear wherever they go. The promised elephant corridors linking habitats have not happened. The promised monitoring of projects that will affect existing corridors has not happened and the promised compensation for damages of personal property has not happened either.

The forest department, when confronted, blamed the mining operations saying that it was unchecked and creating chaos. They also admitted that they did not have the men or the resources to deal with the matter.

So it was a bizarre merry-go-round of blame.

Surely there can be corporate accountability? Surely some places and certain natural wonders are sacred and essential to our survival and deserve to be protected? Surely mining companies can be penalised for violating elephant corridors or operating illegally and polluting the environment? Surely transparent environment assessments can be done so that we can help India grow without destroying all that is precious. Orissa's mining industry is worth 6000 crore. While there is huge enviormental damage and lot of indigenous people have been displaced and lost their land … they do not even see 1 per cent of the profit.

In the next decade we are going to face water shortage, severely depleted forests and inclement weather. By removing and destroying some of the greatest architects of nature – the elephants – we are jeopardizing the life of those forests. By allowing one group of disenfranchised people to bear the brunt of progress, we are losing our humanity. By blithely living as blind consumers without a conscience, we are engineering our own downfall. The forests are key to our survival as a species. There is an old Indian saying, '*jungle nadi ki maa hain*' which does not take rocket science to understand.

Our big cats are dying out. Our glaciers are receding. Every year freak floods and droughts ravage the country. We have lost more habitat space in the '90s than we had in the last hundred years. Our population grows unchecked and the divide between rich and poor grows greater, destabilising us.

We are worried about terrorism and Naxalites. Wait till global warming hits us in earnest. So far the wake-up call is still not clear because the chaos is yet to hit the city streets. When it does it will be too late.

The man-elephant conflict in Orissa is just a microcosmic snapshot of a larger phenomenon. The phenomenon of apathy and inaction; the phenomenon of blaming everyone but ourselves for the problems we face and worse yet, pretending that there is no problem at all.

We need to find the political will, we need to find our humanity, we need to finally understand that ours is a world of finite resources and we are at the tipping point.

On my last night in Orissa, I watched a baby elephant cry over his mother's corpse and refused to be removed from her side. We are in an India today that has this next decade to change course and minimise damage. It could be our last chance.

Umashankar Singh

Umashankar Singh, 36, is
Senior Special Correspondent,
NDTV India.

[It was the murder of four people in Bundelkhand that brought the magnitude of the region's water crisis into the national consciousness. The water wars in Madhya Pradesh had resulted in looting, riots and murder.]

BUNDELKHAND: MURDER FOR WATER

Personal Account

It's 5 o' clock in the morning. My mobile phone rings. Half-asleep, I take the call. It's my Bureau Chief, Manoranjan Bharti. Still half-asleep, I ask, 'Yes Baba?' He tells me: 'You have to go to Hamirpur. There's been a murder for water there. Leave as soon as possible.'

My wife packs my bag as I get ready. Within an hour I am in office. Now the problem is to organise train tickets. Finally, we – cameraman Prem Singh is accompanying me – get tickets to board the evening train.

This incident dates back to August 2007. A few months ago I had covered the Uttar Pradesh Assembly elections. While staying at Kanpur for a fortnight I had travelled as far as Mahoba. Hence, I knew where exactly Hamirpur was. I knew that the road from Kanpur to Hamirpur was nothing but a crater. To reach the spot as soon as possible, I had requested our Kanpur correspondent Arun Agrawal for a vehicle at the railway station. The car was ready when we arrived. Our driver had no clue about the route. However, as I always carry a map for such shoots, it came in handy and I started guiding the driver. Thanks to bad roads, it was almost evening by the time we reached Hamirpur. But our destination was even further: Maudaha municipal limits and from there to Sisolar village – the site of the murder. Once in Hamirpur, we took with us our local colleague Salauddin sahab. The aim was to reach the spot without any delay.

The sun was about to set. The horizon had turned crimson. The road was bad. Nevertheless, we were moving very fast. We were about to reach the village when I spotted the reflection of the setting sun in the murky waters of a pothole. The reflection had turned the water red. I stopped the car and asked Prem to quickly take some shots. An astonished Prem looked at me almost asking, 'You skipped lunch to reach the spot as soon as possible and we haven't as yet reached the place, so what are we going to do with these shots?' I understood his confusion. I told him: 'My dear friend, this will be the last shot of my story. And the script will say: "If we do not wake up even now, every evening Bundelkhand's water will turn red."' Prem understood the significance. Two-three shots and we were on the move again. Just then we saw police vehicles in front of us – the SP and his caravan. I stopped the vehicles and requested the SP to alight from his car. He came out of the vehicle. I read his name on the badge – Nachiketa Jha. Without wasting a moment, I gave him the mike. He was brief in his description of the crime. By now I had collected information pertaining to the crime from Salauddin sahab, and so I could grill the SP. A man had shot dead four of his neighbours. The issue was drawing water from a handpump. There was a difference of time between the first and the fourth murder. So why didn't the police reach the spot on time? At least two lives could have been saved had the police reached on time. The SP was perturbed and insisted that

With no water recharging, the groundwater level is constantly declining leading to villagers travelling miles for this basic amenity.

the police was indeed on time. The minute the camera stopped rolling, he sat in his car and left.

In a couple of minutes we were standing near the handpump at Sisolar village where four people had been killed due to a 'water' dispute. There were policemen deployed at the spot. We started shooting from each and every angle possible – from water dripping from the handpump to the blood trail around the spot.

Some people had gathered at the spot. Among them was Pushpendra, a 17-18-year-old boy, who was a witness to the crime. Sobbing uncontrollably he told us how his grandfather Mangal Singh and uncles Jitendra Singh and Yogendra Singh were shot dead. Their neighbour, Sukhchandan, who had come to pacify the people involved, was also shot dead. The family was grief-stricken. Jitendra and Yogendra's children were too young to understand what had happened; they were curiously looking at our camera. The accused, Randhir Singh, and his family didn't want anyone to draw water from the handpump installed in their premises. Despite being in police custody, Randhir had no regrets. With no remorse in his voice, he said, 'They were not letting the rainwater to flow out. We protested and they came to kill us. I pulled the trigger and murdered them. That's all.' As I was gathering information at the spot of the crime, I realised this wasn't a mere TV story: we needed to see and show all aspects of the issue. Hence, we spoke to everyone present and recorded every angle possible. For instance, one person told us that if you want the government handpump installed within your premises, you have to pay Rs 2,000 as bribe. And once the government employee installs the handpump, the water from that handpump is yours alone. To ensure that others do not get to draw water from that particular handpump you can either remove the handle or lock it with an iron chain.

By this time, it was dark and we decided to return the next morning. The question was where to spend the night. It wasn't possible to return to Kanpur. Going back to Hamirpur would have taken one-and-a-half to two hours, which, in turn, meant the same time would be spent commuting from Hamirpur to the village in the morning. I decided to travel to Maudaha that was only half-an-hour away and spend the night there. Salauddin sahab told me that there were no hotels there. I asked him if there were any

In most villages of the region, Dalits are not even allowed to draw water from the common village well.

alternate accommodation available. He said there was a two-room government guesthouse and we could try there. In case there weren't any guests we could possibly be allowed to stay there.

I thought it would not be appropriate to take help from the local administration. I conveyed this to him. Salauddin sahab explained that there was nothing unethical about staying in a government guesthouse. After all, it had been built with the money that we paid as taxes; besides, we had come here with a positive motive. Our aim was to expose how people were turning into bloodthirsty beasts for water even as the local administration and the state government preferred not to take the situation seriously. I agreed with him. There were no guests staying there and after talking to the concerned official, Salauddin sahab got us both the rooms.

We had barely entered our rooms when local journalists, including representatives of various news channels, reached the guesthouse. They said, 'Why have you come all the way from Delhi? Had you called us we would have sent all possible shots to your office. Anyway, now that you have come here, relax, we have all shots ready. If you want we can give you some transfers or you can even take the tapes… .'

They were all out to show their goodwill. I politely declined and told them: 'Dear friends, I appreciate you offers of help. But now that I am here I would like to understand all aspects of the story

Illegal mining and crushing of stones add to the woes of poor villagers.

on my own, record it and only then leave for Delhi. Of course, whenever I need your help, I will approach you.' Then I asked them all the various queries that I had been mentally noting down throughout the day – from the geological reasons for scarcity of water to why it was being overlooked by the government.

We spent the night somehow in the guesthouse without electricity. I had by then changed my earlier plan of visiting the village in the morning. We had already gathered adequate information from the site of crime. Now, the story had to be taken forward. The problem was to acquaint myself with every aspect of the issue and present the issue in its totality for our audience. I decided to travel as much as possible so that my report was comprehensive.

We visited village after village. We got to know that in certain villages the scarcity of water was so severe that no one wanted to marry off their daughters to those staying in those areas. Marrying off your daughter to those villages meant she would have to walk very long distances every day to fetch water – it amounted to subjecting her to severe hardships. I decided to visit one such village. Sallauddin sahab warned me that to reach any such village I would have to walk at least three to four kilometres. I agreed.

We went up to the dry riverbed of Chandraval and saw women and girls digging up the riverbed. Whatever water they could manage to dig out was being filled in small bowls and poured into buckets and pots. These women from Gora and Khanna villages end up walking 10-12 kilometres everyday in search of water. No wonder no one marries off their daughters in these villages.

While returning from Chandraval riverbed, we saw barren land with cracks. In Jigni village these cracks were a few feet deep and wide. The ground underneath was shifting. The reason was illegal mining of hills and crushing of stones. After capturing these cracks in our camera, we also shot illegal mining activity. The people employed by the mining mafia had seen us, but we managed to get out of the place without any hindrance.

Instead of speaking to a well-known geologist based at Delhi, Mumbai or Kolkata, I decided to speak to a local geologist who might have closely observed the problem. With a little effort we got an interview with a local geologist, JP Vishwakarma. To understand the difficulty in water recharging I interacted with a local official, Ripudaman Singh. With his help I filmed the technique of measuring groundwater and the nitty gritty pertaining to it. Unhesitant in his admission, he told me flouting government's orders, even government buildings were not making any arrangement for water harvesting. With no water recharging, the groundwater level was constantly declining. That's the reason even handpumps were quickly running dry. Around this time we noticed school children having their mid-day meals. We stopped to find out what kind of water was being used to prepare the meal. Shockingly, we came to know that it was from the local pond where animals bathe and also drink water.

As I was travelling through the area, at every nook and corner I could see a new aspect of the issue. At Kapsa village, a priest had covered the handpump installed within the four walls of a temple. In another village, the Dalits could draw water from the well only if the Thakurs allowed them to do so. Scarcity of water for irrigation had led to drought in the fields. The animals were dying. Unfortunately, there was not a single instance of the government trying to solve the crisis.

From morning till evening we continued shooting every aspect of the issue. We listened to the official side of the story regarding putting handpumps under lock and key and the success and failure of various government schemes.

After working on the story for one-and-a-half day, we were

back at the guesthouse for the night. Next evening we had to catch a train from Kanpur. I had gathered enough information and first-hand experience to weave a report and accordingly the next morning I recorded my links. Before returning I visited the site of crime one last time. Seeing cops armed with 3.3 rifles I recorded on camera: 'To stop the third world war on water, cops have been deployed here armed with Second World War weapons. We don't know till how long can they manage to stop it… .'

We rushed to Kanpur and faced the same trouble of getting train tickets, but somehow managed it. I called up Manoranjan Bharti, 'I am on my way back.' He asked me to write the script in the train itself.

The only thing left was video editing. After reaching Delhi, we completed that in as little time as possible. The story was aired on 17 August 2007. It was my first special report on NDTV. I also want to thank my colleague Kadambini Sharma who translated the script into English.

Vaishali Sood

Vaishali Sood is Associate
Features Editor, CNN-IBN.

[Vaishali Sood exposes the underbelly of the glamour industry. She reveals exploitation in Bollywood featuring the line workers like spot boys, production crew and extras as well as musicians and actors.]

THE 70 MM MYTH
Personal Account

It was 2004. I was sitting with my friend Rajeev Masand having a passionate discussion on films. Out of the blue he makes the offer. He tells me he is going to be the Entertainment Editor for CNN-IBN and if I would like to be the producer for the channel's entertainment programming.

Just three-and-a-half years earlier I had scoffed at the very idea. I didn't major in political science from Delhi University and mastered in International Relations from Jawaharlal Nehru University to be an entertainment journalist! My first job in the broadcast media and I was given little choice and put in the team that broadly covered lifestyle and entertainment. For six months I complained, I nagged, I hated my bosses. What were they thinking? I was fresh out of JNU and I wanted to be taken seriously as a journalist.

A category broadly called entertainment journalism is at the very bottom of what most young aspiring journalists want to be. In journalism schools they dream of doing big exposés, lifting the lid of corruption, bringing down governments, reforming society and what have you. I may not have gone to journalism school, but I dreamed those dreams.

And here I was, after three years of trying to find my feet in 'serious' news, accepting the offer of becoming the producer for a guy who wrote about Bollywood! I had been living in Mumbai for a year and was fascinated by the industry. I loved Bollywood and I was no longer going to pretend otherwise.

Part of my job meant I had to produce the daily entertainment show. We had a choice – make it a gossip heavy, salacious show, or tell real, meaningful stories about the business of the entertainment industry. We put our heart and soul into it – putting out stories about how films are made, extensive reports on new cinematic techniques, the business models of smaller films, new revenue streams for feature films, interviews with directors, musicians, scriptwriters and technicians apart from actors and actresses. We covered the premieres of big budget films with all the accompanying fanfare, but we also made sure we featured stories on smaller budget films with interesting themes that were breaking new ground. We interviewed the biggest stars, but we also interviewed the offbeat talents.

Bollywood is full of wonderful stories, and our job as journalists was to bring those stories to you.

But we soon realised that while we were talking about the beautiful and the glitzy, perhaps we were doing a disservice to our audience by not talking about the not-so-glamorous, the not-so-polished, the gray.

For every star who makes it, there are a million who have to satisfy themselves with the role of junior artistes or 'extras' as they're popularly known. Some don't even get that far, destined to a life of complete anonymity. There are a lucky few who will catch a break and make it to television. The rest will keep trying, heartbreak after heartbreak. Others will go back to their day jobs, letting go of their dreams.

We once did a story on a popular café in Versova. You walk in and you'll see a whole lot of very good looking young men and women hanging around. The café is often frequented by the film folk. Who knows when they'll get noticed?

The idea of doing the show *The 70mm Myth* came up very randomly. My boss in Delhi drew up a list of important days. My name was listed next to 1 May, Labour Day. I was to produce a show on Labour Day, but what did I know about the subject? After all, I was an entertainment producer now!

My wonderful team of reporters – Somen Mishra, Vasha Pillai, Archita Kashyap, Priya Krishnamoorthy and my assistant producer Shveta Puranik – we got talking and decided to do our very own exposé. It was our chance to be 'serious' journalists finally.

The first story we did was about below-the-line workers – the light guy, the stuntman, the chai wala. All unit hands who get the raw end of the deal. They work on big-budget films, where crores are spent on sets and costumes and locations. But little attention is paid to the safety of unit hands. Basic facilities like an ambulance on the set, first-aid kits are missing. Accidents happen, people die, and their story rarely makes it to the front pages of the newspaper.

We met Sambhavana Seth. This was before her *Big Boss* fame. She was recognised then as an item girl in Bhojpuri cinema. She had made it. She wasn't at the top of the Bollywood ladder. Not even close. But she was the toast of Bhojpuri films and she was happy she no longer had to knock on doors to beg for roles or ward off advances from sleazy financers who promised her big things.

Sexism in Bollywood? Now isn't that an open secret! Most actresses will get paid a quarter of their male counterparts. Rarely will a film be written with them as central characters. But who wants to admit it? We were pleasantly surprised with the newer crop of actresses making their views known.

We met scriptwriters who dream of seeing their original scripts translating on the big screen. Only to be handed a DVD of a Korean or a Spanish film and asked to add just the right amount of Bollywood masala. Anurag Kashyap and Anjum Rajabali are at the top of their game, perhaps the most well-paid scriptwriters in the industry. And even they get the raw end of the deal at times, left with a mangled version of what they originally wrote now translated into atrocious potboilers.

We met musicians at the mercy of producers and music companies, with no rights to their own creations. Royalty is almost a cuss word for the industry bosses. The new breed of singers and composers are now battling to get their rights restored. Shankar-Ehsaan-Loy, Vishal-Shekar are at the forefront of this campaign.

But while we were doing these stories, we also realised that there is a change happening in Bollywood. The industry is realising that if it needs to be successful, it needs to treat its people fair. Corporates are coming in and bring with them some level of professionalism.

In the end we had to admit to ourselves our show, *The 70 mm Myth*, was not quite an exposé.

The reason we chose to do this show was because we love the industry. My team of reporters and I, all of us were passionate about films and while it was important to talk about the fun, the good, the glitzy, it is just as important to talk about what was not right, with the intention of somewhere making things better for those who form the core of it.

Why was I an entertainment journalist, prepared to be scoffed at by my more high-brow peers? Well, because I loved the movies.

I no longer work with the entertainment team. I moved to Delhi for personal reasons and I now produce health, lifestyle and other features shows. But I'll always miss the excitement of being an 'entertainment' journalist – the initial days when the fan in me would take over the journalist in me – my hands shaking as I put a lapel mike on Amitabh Bachchan's collar, my heart skipping a beat while entering John Abraham's home, being floored by Aamir Khan's intellect; to the later days when I was more irreverent to the people, more keenly focused on telling the stories that mattered.

Even if I don't work on entertainment shows anymore, I'm satisfied that *The 70 mm Myth* was produced for the right reasons. That it won the prestigious Ramnath Goenka Award and I'm writing this today, is validation that important stories must be told. And if they're told honestly and engagingly, they will be heard.

I am deeply indebted to my excellent team that made *The 70 mm Myth* possible. Without their passion and commitment, the show would never have seen the light of day. The award is as much theirs as it is mine.

VK Shashikumar

VK Shashikumar, 38, is the founder of Mediagrove. He was Senior Editor, CNN-IBN, when he won this award for a story done by the Special Investigation Team.

[There are so many stories of the 'hidden wars' in India's northeast remain untold. In this context VK Shashikumar interviewed United National Liberation Front chairman Sanayaima, a first ever interview, and brought to the fore the fact that Manipur had a serious insurgency problem.]

INDIA'S HIDDEN WARS
Personal Account

India's Hidden Wars was conceived as series of on-the-spot reports from the insurgent camps of the rebel groups in India's Northeast. It was planned as a series of reports in which the reporter, in a metaphorical sense, simply held up a mirror and reflected the ground realities. It was an attempt to inform viewers about the extent and scale of the many insurgencies in India's forgotten Northeast.

The core material of my reportage was based on interviews with cadres and leaders of various insurgent groups in their mountain-jungle hideouts and camps in Manipur, Nagaland, Assam and along the India-Myanmar border. Along with my team – video journalist Rajesh Bhardwaj and producer Rohit Khanna – I trekked in this region, visiting and living in the jungle camps of five different rebel groups during a month-long assignment in 2006.

At the United National Liberation Front (UNLF) camp on the Khengjoi hill range in Manipur's Chandel district bordering Myanmar, the UNLF chief, Sanayaima, revealed his plans for a Manipuri people's movement or uprising called Utop Lan. 'There will be some sort of Intifada. That is part of the strategy. Another part of the strategy is to tell the world that something is happening here and you are morally obliged to come to our help. India should not be allowed to simply massacre our people.'

The UNLF's rebellion against the Indian state began in 1964. It now plans to take the war out of the jungles and into the streets of Manipur by sparking civil unrest. Sanayaima says the people's support is what will make the uprising successful. 'If you take our population into consideration and take India's deployment, then

50,000-55,000 security personnel pitted against about 2 million people is nothing.'

This was an assignment I had been planning since February 2006. Finally, in the first week of May I got a message that the UNLF/MPA (Manipur People's Army) leadership was willing to meet us in the second week of May. The destination was 130 kilometres southeast of Imphal along the India-Myanmar border. When we met up with the MPA cadres they radioed back to one of their base camps: 'Thirteen sacks of rice have arrived. Out of the lot, one weighs two quintal.' Later we realised that the thirteen sacks was a code word for journalists and the sack weighing two quintal was a code word for our portly producer, Rohit Khanna!

There were incredible moments during this assignment. We were in a territory completely under the control of the MPA, we trekked through opium fields high up in the mountains, came across various ethnicities including the Burmese. It was a four-day trek to reach one of the base camps of UNLF/MPA. Over these four days we had leeches all over our body. In fact, on the third day, I collapsed and woke up in a hut somewhere in a mountainous village with strangers trying to pull out leeches from my legs and

National media often does not highlight the incidences of violence in the Northeast (especially in Manipur). Statistics show that the conflict between Indian security forces and the insurgent groups in Manipur has taken a heavier toll of human life than in J&K.

The Kuki National Organisation (KNO) has a 1,500 strong force supported by an array of weapons.

eyelids by sprinkling salt or burning them with match sticks. It was one of my most memorable assignments.

The violence in Manipur often goes unreported in the media outside the state. Statistics show that the conflict between Indian security forces and the insurgent groups in Manipur has taken a heavier toll of human life than in Jammu & Kashmir. How many in the rest of India know about Sanayaima, a post-graduate in international relations from Jadavpur University, Kolkata? While interviewing Sanayaima, I realised that my favourite teacher in the university was his favourite as well! Who knows about his insurgent group's four-point proposal for a plebiscite in Manipur? Sanayaima told me that he knows New Delhi will reject his proposal and this will make civil groups trigger a mass uprising. 'The movement is gaining momentum and people in different places are holding meetings and discussions for plebiscite.'

I interacted and interviewed the top leadership of the Nationalist Socialist Council Nagalim (Isak-Muivah), an insurgent group in the northeastern state of Nagaland at Camp Hebron and Mount Gilead camps of the NSCN (IM). The leadership of NSCN (IM) revealed their proposal for a new federal arrangement which made a splash in the region and in the corridors of power in New Delhi. 'We have proposed to the Government of India to work out an agreement that allows these two nations – India and Nagaland – to remain as inseparable entities. Two nations bound together with that special agreement but with respective identities,' said General VS Atem, Special Emissary to collective leadership of National Socialist Council of Nagalim, Isak Muivah (NSCN-IM).

I was given an exclusive access to the insurgent group's Hebron and Mount Gilead camps in Nagaland. NSCN (IM) has been engaged in a cease-fire with the GoI for a decade. The president of Naga Ho Ho, an apex Naga tribal body, has also come out in support of the NSCN (IM) proposal. Keviletus Kiewhuo, in his interview said, 'A new dimension has to come up where it makes Nagas a part of India and India a part of Nagaland. Where both become inseparable and sovereign instead of being a one nation state and quarrel over it.'

It was during my interaction with the NSCN (IM) leadership that a four-point proposal to make peace with India was proposed.

1. India and Nagaland will remain inseparable entities
2. A special constitutional arrangement will cement this federal arrangement
3. The Nagas will manage their own law and order, and local economy
4. While foreign affairs, currency, banking and defence will remain with India

The subtext of TV news documentary and series of stories, *India's Hidden Wars*, is the urgent need to rethink and renew the idea of a truly federal India. This imperative is readily visible in the political aspirations of the Kukis who desire for a settlement within the bounds of the Indian constitution. For months I had worked with intermediaries to secure access to the jungle camps of the Kuki National Organisation (KNO) in south-eastern Manipur and on the India-Myanmar border. The KNO has a 1,500 strong force supported by an array of weapons. Major DJ Haokip of the KNO said, 'At present we use AK-47, M16, DC and mortar is 60 mm.' The armed wing of the KNO has created under a ceasefire agreement with the Indian Army since August 2005 and is a product of Manipur's ethnic wars. 'If India wants us to be part of the Indian Union we are happy to do that. Then recognise our territory by way of statehood,' said Seilen Hoakip, spokesperson of KNO.

India's Hidden Wars attempted to sensitively unravel why India's Northeast is such a boiling pot of ethnic hostilities. Through exclusive interviews and field reports, it sought to explain why the United National Liberation Front (UNLF) – Manipur's largest, active and primarily Meitei insurgent group – is fighting for an 'Independent Manipur' and so, is violently opposed to the Kukis. The third player is the National Socialist Council of Nagaland (Isak Muivah) or the NSCN (IM) which is involved in a brutal ethnic war with the Kukis because both claim Manipur's hill districts. The NSCN (IM) wants integration of these districts to form Greater Nagaland. But unlike the UNLF and the NSCN (IM), the armed wing of the KNO has adopted a pro-India stance. This allows them to carry arms and to keep on training despite the ceasefire. The Kuki militia does what the army can't – protect Kuki villages from the UNLF and NSCN (IM). 'The Kukis, the KNO's objective is to find solutions within the framework of the Indian Constitution. We firmly believe in being Indian,' said Hoakip.

India's Hidden Wars also focused on the various insurgent and terror groups in Assam. It profiled the DHD group in Karbi Anglong and the Bodos. In fact, I spent considerable time in the National Democratic Front for Bodoland (NDFB) camps in Assam and interviewed the group's leaders on their demand for a 'Bodoland'. 'We are still strong enough. We can, if we want to, strike India. We can damage India with resources and power,' said Basumatari Swmkhwr, alias Govinda Basumatary, general secretary of NDFB. Despite being in a ceasefire with the government since May 2005, Bodo insurgents continue to learn guerilla warfare tactics and their hopes for an independent Bodo state are indeed alive.

India's Hidden Wars will always remain one of my toughest and in-depth assignments that examined the insurgency movements in India's Northeast. It successfully documented the aspirations of various communities in the region and attempted to be the window to a world that mainstream India is often cut off from. In the final analysis this reportage intended to be a mirror that reflected the ground realities in the insurgency affected northeastern region with accuracy, honesty and sensitivity.